KEYS TO INCORPORATING

Steven A. Fox, LL.M., C.P.A.
Attorney-at-Law
Palm Beach, Florida

New York • London • Toronto • Sydney

All inquiries should be addressed to:
Barron's Educational Series, Inc.
250 Wireless Boulevard
Hauppauge, New York 11788

Library of Congress Catalog Card No. 88-34621

International Standard Book No. 0-8120-3973-4

Library of Congress Cataloging in Publication Data

Fox, Steven A.
  Keys to incorporating.
  Includes index.
  ISBN 0-8120-3973-4
  1. Incorporation—United States.   2. Corporation law—United
States.   3. Corporations—Taxation—Law and legislation—United
States.   I. Title. II. Series.
KF1420.F69   1989
346.73'06622—dc 19
[347.3066622]   88-34621

CONTENTS

1

INTRODUCTION TO BUSINESS ORGANIZATION

Selecting the form of doing business is one of the first decisions the owner of an enterprise must make. Should the business be a proprietorship, a partnership, or a corporation? Even after the choice has been made, circumstances may trigger a change in the nature of the business, so that the best form at one time may not be the best at another.

The basis for making a sensible choice of business form rests on commercial law and tax regulations, which are different in their effects on the various forms of doing business. An initial consideration is whether the enterprise is to be a not-for-profit concern or a for-profit-concern. This book concentrates on the latter category.

Broadly speaking, the forms of for-profit enterprise in the United States can be divided into two areas, noncorporate and corporate. Principal noncorporate forms include the sole proprietorship, the general partnership, and the limited partnership. The corporate forms may be divided into regular (C) corporations and S corporations. The distinction between regular and S corporations is an important one, relating to two subchapters of the federal tax law applying different tax treatment to closely held businesses than that for other corporate enterprises. (See Key 21/S CORPORATIONS.)

Other classifications of for-profit entities exist as well, such as the land trust and the Massachusetts business trust. However, for purposes of space, only the major types will be considered in this book. One special classification, the professional corporation, will be discussed separately because of the growing interest in the subject recently (see Key 27).

The *sole proprietorship* is the noncorporate form for a business having only one owner. It represents the simplest and most inexpensive form to organize, operate, and terminate, but it is inconvenient to transfer to another owner. Since the sole proprietorship and its owner are identical for tax and nontax purposes, the proprietor has *unlimited liability* for the obligations of the business. Although federal tax law requires the sole proprietor to maintain separate books and records for the business, all federal income tax consequences of the business flow directly to the proprietor.

The general partnership and limited partnership forms are the noncorporate forms for businesses having more than one owner. The Uniform Partnership Act (UPA) provides that a partnership is an association of two or more persons to carry on as co-owners for profit. Partnerships are basically of two types — commercial partnerships and personal service partnerships. In the latter, there is rarely any substantial inventory or fixed assets, since the income of the enterprise is derived from the services rendered by the partners. A general partnership lacks continuity of life, centralization of management, and free transferability of interests, although the partnership agreement may allow for some of these characteristics.

In the general partnership, the general partners have

6

unlimited liability for the debts and obligations of the partners. In a limited partnership, a specified group of partners — called the limited partners — may invest their money and share in the returns while limiting their liability to the amount of their contributions. In any partnership there must be at least one general partner. It is important to note that the limited partners, unlike general partners, lack decisional authority. In fact, if limited partners exercise any control over the business, they lose their special limited-liability status. From an organizational standpoint, the principal difference between the general and the limited partnership is that a general partnership is a means for carrying on an operating business while the limited partnership is largely an investment vehicle.

A partnership is not a taxable entity but must determine its profit or loss and file an "information return" on Form 1065. Since no tax is paid by the partnership, the partners are taxed as individuals on their *distributive* shares of partnership taxable income, whether they have actually received the cash or not.

A business in a corporate form is generally treated as a separate entity for both tax and nontax purposes. The income of a regular (C) corporation may be taxed first to the corporation, then to the shareholders as dividends, and, with the passage of the Tax Reform Act of 1986, again at both the corporate and shareholder levels on liquidation. This should be contrasted with the S corporation, which has most of the characteristics of a C corporation but is generally not treated as a separate taxable entity. Thus, the S corporation is a pass-through somewhat akin to the partnership, with items of income, deduction, loss, and credit said to flow through directly to the shareholders.

The corporate form is chosen by many entrepreneurs because of its core attributes — limited liability, continuity of life, centralization of management, and free transferability of interests. *Limited liability* means that the shareholders generally risk no more than their total investment in the business. This can be extremely important. If there is an unanticipated reversal in business conditions that causes a corporation to start losing money and, perhaps eventually, to default on its loans, the shareholders are not held personally liable to make good on those losses and loans.

Continuity of life refers to the fact that corporations are generally established with perpetual existence. Thus, the death, disability, or withdrawal of a shareholder — even the controlling shareholder — will not necessarily terminate corporate existence. A corporation offers *centralization of management* in that the board of directors has exclusive authority to make management and business decisions on behalf of the corporation. (A limited partnership generally possesses this attribute, too, in that the general partners have continuing exclusive authority to make management and business decisions.) Corporate shares of stock are often more *freely transferred* than are partnership interests. However, in corporations owned and managed by a relatively small number of persons (known as closely held corporations), shares may not be disposed of easily if there is no ready market for the securities and if the shares are subject to restrictions on transferability.

This book will focus on the role of the closely held corporation, which is becoming a form of choice for the small businessperson. In particular the advantages and disadvantages of the S corporation will be described and evaluated. This book will also consider a special form of closely held corporation, the professional corporation. State laws authorize the formation of corporations to render professional services such as medicine, dentistry, and accounting. All the shareholders (and generally all the directors and officers) must be licensed to practice the particular profession in the state.

Incorporation is governed by individual state laws, among which there is considerable variation. Fortunately, most states follow either the Model Business Corporation Act ("MBCA") or, more recently, the revised version ("RMBCA"). Thus, most of the explanations in the keys that follow will be based on these models. Corporate formalities as prescribed by law must be observed in even the smallest corporations. It is important for entrepreneurs and owners to understand that the corporation is a separate entity, governed not only by governmental laws and regulations but also by its own articles of incorporation and bylaws. A corporation may enter into contracts in its own name, hold, convey, and receive property, and sue and be sued. In the federal courts, a corporation is deemed to be a citizen in the state in which it has its principal place of business as well as in the state in which it is incorporated.

A word of caution is in order here. Much of the popular writing about incorporation reflects a belief in do-it-yourself incorporating. Indeed, many business owners have successfully formed their own corporations. Although small businesspersons and professionals are understandably cautious about expending unnecessary funds for advice, the fact is that obtaining legal, tax, and other advice is a sound investment.

As an example, although everything may appear to be in order when the parties are in the process of forming their business, personality conflicts and other differences of opinion can lead to dissension within the business and outright deadlock. Disinterested outside advisers have the experience to anticipate such problems so that appropriate action can be taken before it's too late.

This book is not intended as a substitute for legal, tax, or other advice that might be obtained from qualified advisers familiar with your individual needs and your jurisdiction's requirements. Rather, it is designed to frame the issues in such a way as to make the best use of your time with any advisers you engage. This book will not make you an instant expert, but it will give you a great deal of practical information on issues of particular relevance to your situation.

2

THE INCORPORATION PROCESS

This key is intended to present an overview of the incorporation process and some related federal and state laws. The emphasis will be on the attorney-client relationship.

Businesspeople interested in incorporation should meet with an attorney in a preincorporation conference. Provisions of the articles of incorporation ("articles") and other instruments required by law are discussed to ensure that their content is fully understood by all concerned. If there is more than one principal involved, is the attorney representing the majority interest, the minority interest, or both? There is a potential conflict of interest here.

An initial consideration is the proposed name for the corporation. This is an important step. It is worth noting that filing the approved name in the articles with the secretary of state's office does not imply that the use of a name will not violate some other law. (See Key 6.)

The next consideration is whether a preincorporation agreement or subscription agreement should be adopted by the parties. A preincorporation agreement is simply a contract to create a corporation, while a subscription agreement is a contract for the purchase of corporate stock. These two agreements may be combined into one. There is a great deal of ground to be covered in a preincorporation agreement. First, the contracting parties state that the corporation will be formed under and pursuant to state law, then they indicate what the name, purposes, duration, and registered office and agent of the corporation will be, the fact that the corporation will be under the management of a board of directors ("board"), what capital contributions/loans will be made, how much the authorized capital stock will be, and who shall be the incorporator(s). The function of the incorporator(s) is a formality; in fact, an incorporator has no authority and no duties other than to sign the corporate articles. Other points that should be covered in the preincorporation agreement are whether cumulative voting and preemptive rights will be permitted; whether the corporation agrees to indemnify directors and/or officers against errors and omissions committed by them; who the initial shareholders will be and their respective share ownership; Section 1244 implications; whether the board or shareholders can act without a meeting; what expenses incurred qualify for reimbursement; whether there will be a covenant not to compete (even where permitted by state law, such covenants must be reasonable as to time and area); what will happen in the event of corporate deadlock; where the principal offices of the business will be located; and how the agreement may be terminated.

In a subscription agreement, the prospective shareholders — known as the subscribers — each promise to purchase a specified amount of stock from the corporation for a specified price. (In some states, an incorporator must subscribe to at least one share.) Such an agreement may be executed before or after the corporation is formed and is generally irrevocable for six months, except by consent of all subscribers or as otherwise provided in the agreement. It is good practice nevertheless that the term of the subscription be specified in the agreement. If the amount due under a subscription agreement is not paid when due, the corporation may collect the amount in the same manner as any debt due from a third party debtor. Moreover, the agreement may provide for other penalties.

The next consideration is preparation of the articles of incorporation and bylaws. For the articles there are two types of provisions — mandatory and permissive, or optional. Mandatory provisions include, for example, the corporate name (which must contain a word like corporation to indicate that the enterprise is a corporation); the corporate purpose (e.g., to engage in any activities or business permitted under state law); the registered office and agent; the names and addresses of the initial board of directors; the names and addresses of the incorporators; and the authorized capital, which generally refers to the aggregate number, par value, and class or classes of shares the corporation is authorized to issue. Although par value historically represented the expected selling price of the shares, today, shares may be issued with or without a stated par value. Nevertheless, stock having a par value may not be issued for consideration worth less than the aggregate par value of the issued shares. (See Key 20.)

In addition to the mandatory provisions, the articles may contain virtually any lawful provision that is desirable for regulation of the corporation's internal affairs. Such optional provisions might concern preemptive rights, which allow a shareholder to purchase a sufficient number of shares subsequently issued to preserve his proportionate interest; quorum requirements for meetings; voting requirements (e.g., each outstanding share is entitled to a single vote unless provided otherwise in the articles); the board's ability to fix compensation; director conflicts of interest; whether board meetings may be held by conference phone; whether the officers and directors are entitled to indemnification from the corporation; how directors may be removed; and so on. Many of these provisions may appear instead in the corporate bylaws.

It should be noted that certain objectives cannot be accomplished in the articles. For example, shareholders cannot be excluded from voting on amendment of the articles or on a merger, consolidation, or transfer of all or substantially all of the corporate assets.

If the articles are filed in proper form and are accompanied by the required fees, the secretary of state is generally required to issue a certificate of incorporation. Should the filing be defective or inadequate, the secretary of state is generally obliged to notify the incorporators of the reason for rejection. In some states the secretary of state is required either to accept or to reject the articles not later than the close of the business day following the day of filing.

Once the certificate of incorporation is issued by the secretary of state's office, corporate existence will generally be reckoned as beginning as of the time of delivery of the articles to the secretary of state. Some states may permit the selection of an alternative date. Note that a de jure corporation is formed when there is substantial compliance with all of the mandatory provisions of the incorporation statute, a de facto corporation may result if there was a good faith attempt to organize under an incorporation statute (see Key 10).

The next step is to prepare for the first official meeting of the incorporators. Generally, the incorporators will execute a waiver of notice of the meeting so that the meeting can be held without delay, unless the proper notice was given. At the first meeting and at all subsequent meetings, minutes must be maintained stating when and where the meeting was held, who was present, and who served as chairman and as secretary. Generally, the chairman first calls the meeting to order and the secretary presents and reads the waiver of notice of the meeting. The chairman then reports that the articles were filed in the office of the secretary of state on a specified date and orders that a copy of the certificate of incorporation be inserted in the minute book as part of the official records of the meeting. These are formalities, but they must be followed.

Next, a proposed form of the bylaws for the regulation and management of the affairs of the corporation is read, section by section, and adopted and ordered to be made a part of the permanent records following the certificate of incorporation in the minute book. The board of directors is then elected. As soon as other business is completed, the meeting is adjourned. It is worth mentioning that, subject to state law, a sole incorporator who is also the sole shareholder may file a statement in lieu of holding the organizational meeting.

The next step is to prepare for the initial board of directors meeting. Just as the shareholders did, the directors should execute a waiver of notice of the meeting. Minutes of board meetings must be maintained, reflecting when and where the meeting was held, who was present, and who served as chairman and as secretary. Generally, the chairman first calls the meeting to order and the secretary presents and reads the waiver of notice of the meeting. Various resolutions are then considered and voted on, such as naming the respective officers; approving the corporate seal and the form of stock certificate; acknowledging who will serve as registered agent and where the corporate bank account will be maintained; authorizing the treasurer to pay all fees and expenses incident to incorporation; accepting the contributions of the various shareholders for their shares; in the case of small corporations, deciding that an S election is desirable; considering possible fringe benefit arrangements, many of which (such as medical reimbursement plans) require corporate action; adopting a fiscal year; designating a principal office location; and such other resolutions and issues as are properly brought before the board. (Note: on occasion, the board will be asked to issue what are known as certified resolutions, which conclusively show to third persons dealing with the corporation that the person acting on behalf of the corporation had the necessary authority. Such resolutions may need to be notarized or placed under seal.) Generally, the directors will then sign a ratification of the minutes, stating that they ratify, approve, and confirm all that transpired at the meeting, the minutes having been read and approved. Note that in lieu of holding a board meeting, it may be possible to take action by the unanimous written consent of the directors.

The corporate bylaws may also be adopted at the initial meeting of the board. While the articles may be viewed as the corporation's "constitution," the bylaws may be seen as internal administrative regulations for carrying on the enterprise. The bylaws cover a broad range of matters such as the date of the annual meetings, board size, officer authority and duties, board and shareholder meeting notices, places of such meetings, quorum requirements, and indemnification provisions. Although it is possible to include a broad range of items in the bylaws, such provisions must not be inconsistent with the articles or with state law. Further, the power to adopt, alter, or repeal the bylaws following the organizational meeting rests with the board unless the power is reserved exclusively to the shareholders by the articles or in bylaws previously adopted by the shareholders. Since the bylaws are not a matter of public record like the articles, generally, they cannot bind transactions with nonshareholder third parties.

Once the initial directors of the corporation have completed the organizational meeting, shares have been issued, and officers have been elected, the various organizational documents should be placed in a record book, to be updated periodically as meetings are held and other actions are taken. A corporate kit available at many stationery stores provides a handy organizer for a corporation's important records. Some attorneys prefer to keep the corporate records at their law office, but this should be decided by the corporation's officers. Ordinarily, a corporate kit will also include a seal, although many jurisdictions do not require that a seal be used on corporate documents. As a practical matter, many banks continue to require the seal on banking resolutions authorized by the corporation.

As a related matter, much of the data required to be on the face of the share certificates can be engraved thereon by the vendor of the corporate kit. Generally, a share certificate must contain the name of the corporation, a statement that the corporation is organized under the laws of the particular state, the class of shares and the designation of the series (if any) that the certificate represents, the par value of the shares (or a statement that the shares are without par value), and other statements, such as a statement that particular shares are nonvoting. Other required information, including the name of the party to whom the certificate is issued and the number of shares the certificate represents, can be filled in by hand as necessary. The president and corporate secretary will generally need to sign each share certificate.

In some cases, there may be restrictions on the trans-

15

ferability of shares (see Key 30). State and federal securities laws require that a restrictive legend be placed on the certificates representing such shares. These exemptions are generally available for closely-held corporations. However, to ensure that these exemptions will be held legal and valid, each shareholder should send an investment letter to the corporation indicating that he is purchasing the shares for investment for his own account, acknowledging the restrictions placed on subsequent transfers under federal and state securities law, and agreeing not to transfer the shares in violation of such restrictions. State law may require that a notice of the transaction be filed with the state and a fee paid. The corporate kit will contain not only share certificates but a share transfer ledger, in which can be entered the names of the shareholders, their respective holdings, from whom the shares were transferred, to whom the shares were transferred, and related information. Each subsequent transfer should be reflected in the ledger.

Corporate records should be correctly maintained and, in general, the corporation should act like a corporation. Otherwise, creditors may be able to sue the owners individually and the IRS may attack the separateness of the corporate form. Formal meetings of the board and of the shareholders called at least as often as required by state law — and formal minutes should be maintained of all meetings. Moreover, the directors and officers should, in their corporate capacity, make prudent decisions respecting compensation, etc., and the corporate name should be used at the entrance to the office and on all stationery, contracts, billing, and business forms. Accounting records should be in the name of the corporation, and in no case should the corporate account be commingled with the personal account of the owner(s). Adherence to corporate formalities may seem burdensome but it is absolutely necessary if the corporation is to continue as a viable entity.

Prior to incorporating, it must be determined whether compliance with provisions of the state's Bulk Transfer Act is indicated. This applies only to existing businesses with inventory and creditors and basically requires that a specified number of days' notice be given to creditors before taking possession of the goods to be purchased or paid for, whichever comes first. For this purpose, the seller must furnish the buyer with a sworn list of the creditors, which generally must be filed with the clerk of the court.

A new corporation may also apply for a corporate employer identification number, filing Form SS-4 with the IRS, and for the small business tax election for S corporations, filing Form 2553 with the IRS. At the state level, application should be made for a sales tax number, since many transactions are subject to the state sales and use tax. In most cases, corporations and other businesses must collect the proper tax on each taxable transaction and periodically forward the money collected to the state. An attorney or accountant generally handles filing these forms.

An attorney may also have to advise whether or not the business will be subject to federal and state unemployment tax. In addition, as far as employees are involved, a number of federal, state, and local laws can be triggered. For example, there are prohibitions against various forms of discrimination; an I-9 Form may need to be completed for the Immigration and Naturalization Service; Occupational Safety and Health Administration ("OSHA") regulations must be observed; the Fair Labor Standards Act ("FLSA") includes requirements that covered employees be paid no less than minimum wage and time and one-half for hours worked in excess of 40 per week; oppressive child-labor practices have been outlawed; and some state right-to-work laws make it unlawful for any person to interfere with the employment of another. Where qualified plans are involved (e.g., pension and profit sharing plans), a host of reporting and disclosure requirements are applicable; fortunately for plans with fewer than 100 employees, a shorter form may be used.

Most employers are subject to state workers' compensation laws, which impose liability on the employer regardless of fault. A policy should be obtained from an insurer authorized to sell workers' compensation insurance in the state. Other types of insurance are important, too. A business should also obtain life insurance on the lives of key employees and perhaps a group life policy as an employee benefit. In order to attract the best employees, a good health insurance program is also a must. The business should consider the applicability of property and liability insurance and take a detailed inventory of what assets might be exposed to loss.

The corporation will be required to file federal and, where applicable, state corporate income tax returns. The IRS requires a host of information statements. For example, each year the employer must prepare a Form W-2 for each employee. There are many different 1099 forms that may need to be prepared. Form 1099-MISC is used to report ordinary kinds of payments made such as rents, royalties, prizes, awards, and nonemployee compensation, while Form 1099-INT is used to report payments of interest to a borrower. Every corporation should develop a tax filing schedule to ensure that it is in compliance with all such requirements. The corporation will be required to withhold and pay over income and social security taxes and to pay any applicable intangible personal property tax.

The locality may also impose a tangible personal property tax, and the state may impose a documentary tax, such as the transfer of shares. If the firm plans to do business in any states other than the state where it has been incorporated, it may subject itself to penalties if it begins such activity before being authorized to do so by the state (see Key 18).

Finally, the corporation will be required to satisfy any zoning or other regulatory requirements and obtain any federal, state, or local licenses. Business licenses may be necessary at both the city and county level. It is important that no contracts or agreements requiring a license be executed until the license or permit is actually obtained. Certain licenses, such as those for the sale of liquor, may require extensive background checks.

3

TYPES OF
CORPORATIONS

Corporations may be classified in a number of different ways — public or private, profit or nonprofit, publicly held or closely held.

The term *public* has two meanings here. Strictly speaking, public corporations are units of government, such as towns, cities, and villages, and governmental agencies, such as the U.S. Postal Service. In common usage, however, public corporations are those companies in which the general public may own, or purchase, shares of common stock. This stock is generally traded — bought and sold — through a stock exchange or on one of the "over-the-counter" markets.

By far the greatest number of corporations in the United States are closely held, whether within a family or among a limited number of shareholders. Shares are not available to the general public. Most of these enterprises are relatively small in size, although some family companies are very large. For instance, the Hearst Corporation would be in the Fortune 500 if its shares were publicly held.

A form of the closely held corporation that has come into increasing favor since the 1986 Tax Reform Act is the S CORPORATION (see Key 21), in which any profits are taxed to the shareholders directly. This is not the case in the regular corporation, which generally pays income taxes on its profits before paying dividends to its shareholders, who then must pay income taxes on these distributions. This amounts to double taxation, and so Congress authorized the S corporation primarily to relieve small businesses from this extra burden. With tax rates now generally higher for corporations than for individuals, S corporations should be the choice of many entrepreneurs starting a new business. Another special category of corporation is the PROFESSIONAL CORPORATION (see Key 16).

Another distinction between corporations is their status as profit or nonprofit. The profit category includes all business corporations whether or not they make money in a given year. Indeed, given the risks of starting a small business, many companies set up as for-profit corporations never make any money during their entire existence. For the most part the nonprofit category of corporations includes clubs, associations, most schools and colleges, charitable and religious organizations, many cooperatives, and other groups. The officers of nonprofit corporations may or may not be paid a salary, but such corporations may never distribute any surplus funds to directors or members. Most nonprofit corporations do not have any stockholders, but all have a governing body such as a board of directors or trustees. Nonprofits should seek to be tax qualified such that contributions may be deducted from income for tax purposes and that any corporate earnings will be exempt from taxation.

4

CLOSELY HELD
VERSUS
PUBLICLY HELD
CORPORATIONS

There are several important distinctions between closely held and publicly held corporations. Although there is no precise definition of what constitutes a closely held (or close or closed or privately held) corporation, generally it is one that is organized in the corporate form and owned and managed by relatively few persons. The "closeness" refers to the relationship of the shareholders, since typically a small group of owners is brought together through family relationships or friendship or mutual business interests. In the case of the publicly held (or public or open) corporation, the shares are owned by a larger, more diverse group and are probably traded either on a securities exchange or over the counter.

Unlike the typical shareholders in a public corporation, who are likely to be simply investors with no intention of assuming any management responsibilities, many shareholders in closely held corporations consider themselves to be active participants in the business. In fact, many such shareholders are employed on a full-time basis by the corporation. The problem is that in the traditional management structure of shareholders, directors, and officers, the corporation, as created by the state, must conform to the statutory norms. This is known as the concession theory and is at odds with the practical reality of the close corporation, where shareholders may wish to agree among themselves as to how the business will be managed.

Depending on the law in one's state of incorporation, close corporations may be subject to the general incorporation law or to specially drafted statutes designed to deal with their particular concerns. Thus, under California law, a corporation with ten or fewer shareholders can elect close-corporation status so that it can operate more or less as an incorporated partnership under a shareholders' agreement, dispensing with many of the corporate formalities. Under Delaware law, the stock of such a close corporation may not be held by more than 30 persons. Additional restrictions are that the corporation's stock will be subject to restraints on transferability and that the corporation will make no public offering of its securities.

California law also holds that "The failure of a close corporation to observe corporate formalities relating to meetings of directors or shareholders in connection with the management of its affairs, pursuant to an agreement ... shall not be considered a factor tending to establish that the shareholders have personal liability for corporate obligations." Although operating on such an informal basis will not subject the shareholders to personal liability for corporate debts, shareholders who assume management responsibility may be subject to liability for management acts or omissions that would otherwise be imposed on directors. In other words, an owner-manager has responsibilities similar to those of a director in a publicly held corporation. Note further that close-corporation statutes vary considerably in terms of the arrangements offered, from enabling shareholders to replace directors by assuming some or all of the management powers to allowing a majority of the shareholders to enter into an enforceable management agreement, to enabling the shareholders to enter into agreements modifying the basic structure and rights of the corporation as to resemble a partnership, to allowing a shareholder (or at least those owning a specified percentage of shares) to force the corporation's legal termination.

The idea of such shareholder agreements is to enable the shareholders to provide for any system of management and control they want. Such a comprehensive agreement may cover such basic matters as employment rights, management and voting rights, deadlock and dissolution, and the transferability of shares. The actual agreement may appear in the articles of incorporation or the bylaws—or they may be free-standing (i.e., contained in a separate document), depending on state law and/or the parties involved. In some states, certain kinds of agreements will be permitted only if they have been included in the articles. In any case, notice of the existence of an agreement should be placed on the stock certificates held by the parties to the agreement. In some states, even a minority of shareholders may enter into such agreements, while other laws offer greater support if all of the shareholders are parties. Even in states where the statutes require that the agreement be located in the articles, some courts have enforced such understandings in unanimous agreements that were not so included.

In terms of the contents of such agreements, they vary widely but often provide for greater-than-majority quorum and voting requirements for both shareholder and board meetings. Such requirements effectively give the minority interests a veto power, which is something akin to the unanimity requirements associated with the partnership form. One might ask why a majority interest would give a minority shareholder such power over corporate affairs. The answer is that power sharing might be necessary in order to attract individuals who might not otherwise participate in the venture. In other cases, an agreement can bring together two or more minority shareholders who together constitute a majority and who wish to ensure that the contracting parties will continue to act together in the future.

Although many of the principles that are applicable to

corporations generally (e.g., matters of corporate finance) do apply to the closely held corporation, the operation of most close corporations resembles more closely the partnership form. Like a partnership, the relationship among the owners must be one of confidence and loyalty. Although courts are looking more closely to determine if majority interests have oppressed the minority shareholders (e.g., by unreasonably withholding dividends), this is not basically the answer. Taking preventive measures, such as inserting provisions for the rights of minority shareholders in the articles of incorporation, offers a much broader guarantee.

As far as publicly held corporations are concerned, with the exception of those who own a controlling interest in a business, the powers of the shareholders are limited to the election of directors, adoption, amendment, or repeal of the bylaws, and the consideration of certain fundamental changes in the corporate structure. Although shareholders may also vote in other specialized actions — such as approving contracts involving interested directors, authorizing indemnification of directors and officers, and authorizing loans to officers — and become involved in some aspects of corporate oversight such as inspecting the corporate books and records under specified circumstances, it is truly the board that actually exercises the corporate powers and is responsible for the management of the business.

In reality, then, both closely held and publicly held corporations may sell shares to raise funds, but shareholders in the former generally participate directly in management, while shareholders in the latter generally leave the management of the business to others. Not surprisingly, therefore, publicly held corporations are subject to a much greater degree of scrutiny concerning their affairs than are closely held corporations.

5

CORPORATE LOCATION

One of the first questions prospective incorporators must answer is, In what state shall we incorporate? As a general rule, a business should be incorporated in the state where its principal place of operation is located. The possible advantages of filing for incorporation outside one's home jurisdiction (such as more favorable taxes or laws, simpler procedures, less pervasive governmental supervision, and the like) typically will be outweighed by the extra cost and trouble associated with out-of-state incorporation.

Although certain states like Delaware have gained a well-deserved reputation as being receptive to the changing needs of business, most states today do offer a modern corporation statute that does not place unreasonable restrictions on operations (be they small business or otherwise). Of course, small businesses located in a metropolitan area that encompasses two or more states might find it worthwhile to investigate the laws in each state. This would be particularly true of a retailer or other business operating in more than one state.

Differences in corporate law among states range from the trivial to the significant. Thus, the states vary as to whether the incorporators must subscribe to stock, and if so, for how much, how many persons must serve as incorporators, and whether partnerships and corporations may themselves act as incorporators. Some states require that a director be a U.S. citizen, and in some states directors must also be shareholders. In some states, directors may be indemnified under the articles, bylaws, or other corporate provisions, while in other states, the indemnification statute is deemed exclusive. In some states, a majority of the directors constitutes a quorum unless the articles or bylaws provide otherwise, while in other states, a quorum may be less than a majority but not less than one third (or at least two) of the total directors. Other states don't mandate such a minimum.

States also vary as to the number of directors required. If there is only one shareholder, state law may authorize a one-person board. But some states require that there be more than one incorporator and director. This makes such states unappealing to entrepreneurs, who prefer to keep initial control of the corporation in their own hands. Under the RMBCA, the number of directors may be specified or fixed in accordance with the articles or bylaws. In terms of voting, state laws vary widely. Thus, in some jurisdictions, the right to vote cannot be denied to any class of shares, thus making it impossible to create nonvoting stock as a means of preserving control. There also may be requirements that set a minimum paid-in capital, and some states provide that par value of the shares may not be less than $1 each. Should a corporation begin doing business before the minimum has been paid in, there may be liability for the difference between the minimum paid-in capital and the amount actually paid in. As far as stock that is issued without par value is concerned, some jurisdictions arbitrarily evaluate no-par for initial tax purposes at $10 to $100 per share, while others do not even authorize the use of no-par shares.

These are but a few of the variations that exist among the states. A detailed analysis of the various state laws can be found in the *Model Business Corporation Act Annotated,* which is available in many county law libraries.

At one point in time an important reason for incorporating

in a state other than the true home state was to avoid service of process, or being subject to legal action. And some business-people without legal experience still believe that in most cases people won't bother to sue or to take other legal action if they have to go out of state to do so. But this is no longer true, because this advantage has been substantially eliminated through the adoption of the so-called long-arm statutes, which effectively permit the courts to exercise jurisdiction based on a variety of corporate actions within the state, such as the commencement of a tort, the making of a contract, or the ownership of property.

Consideration should also be given to any applicable taxes and fees, the business climate, and the relevant case law. To cite an example of one state's structure, under Pennsylvania law, two types of state corporate income taxes are imposed. There is a corporate net income tax, referred to as an excise tax, and a corporation income tax, essentially a property tax that is levied on corporations not subject to the corporate net income tax but which own property or conduct activities in the state. Then there is the state capital stock tax and a franchise tax. Certain types of entities, such as banks, are exempted. Pennsylvania also has a corporate loans tax.

It is worth noting that state corporate income and other taxes may even be assessed on out-of-state corporations so long as such taxation does not discriminate against companies engaged in interstate commerce, does not "unduly burden" interstate commerce, or violate a corporation's right to due process. The taxes or fees must serve a legitimate interest of the state imposing them, and be reasonable in relation to the corporation's activity within the state.

6

CORPORATE NAME

Choosing a name for your corporation is generally simple enough. Of course, there are some practical considerations, such as the appropriateness of the name to the business, its advertising potential, and its availability and protectability. Subject to state law, each name must contain the word "corporation," "incorporated," "limited," or an abbreviated version thereof to indicate that an entity is incorporated. Some states also recognize the use of "company" or "co." as a sufficient indication of corporate status.

After a name has been selected, it must be approved by the state. Here there may be some unforeseen problems because the name may not lawfully be the same as that of another corporation already formed or qualified to do business in the state. Interestingly, the old version of the Model Business Corporation Act did not allow a name that was the same as, or deceptively similar to, any other corporate name — and that is still the law in many states. The Revised Act (RMBCA) requires only that the name be distinguishable upon the records of the secretary of state from any other corporate name. Relatedly, insofar as out-of-state business operations are concerned, generally, no application for authority to transact business in a state may be issued to a corporation unless its name conforms to law.

How can one determine whether a particular name is

available? Generally, the secretary of state's office stores corporate names in a computer that provides immediate access. Subject to state law, name availability can be determined over the counter in the secretary of state's office, by written correspondence, or sometimes over the phone. There may be a charge for checking availability after the first name. There are private companies that can handle this and other parts of the incorporating process. They are often listed in the yellow pages under Incorporating Companies. Typically, an attorney handling an incorporation will ask for a first, second, and a third choice in order of preference. The most prudent will also check other sources since the secretary of state's approval of a name does not protect against a claim that a name's use amounts to a trademark infringement or unfair competition.

Once it is determined that a name is available, it should be reserved. Reservation is especially important if the articles of incorporation are not going to be drafted, executed, and filed soon after availability of the name is established. Anyone intending to form a corporation may reserve a name. The application generally must set forth the name and address of the applicant, the name to be reserved, and the date of reservation. If the secretary of state finds the name applied for is still available, the name generally will be reserved for a nonrenewable period (e.g., 120 days).

There are some additional considerations. In many states, it is forbidden to include in the corporate name such words as insurance and bank unless such use is explicitly permitted by law. The reason is that such firms are regulated by the state so that special licenses — or approvals — are necessary for a corporation to operate in such fields. Further, many corporations will do business under a name that is not the same as the name in the articles. Fictitious-name statutes make it unlawful to do business under such a name without providing public notice of intention to use the name and registering it by filing an affidavit with the clerk of the county where the principal place of business is to be located.

You will need proof of publication of the fictitious name

when you open your corporate bank account. The bank will also want to see the articles of incorporation, corporate seal, employer identification number (or proof that the tax number has been applied for), and of course the corporate resolution authorizing the account. This latter is generally on a bank-provided form. (Caveat: The bank may impose a penalty if the tax number is not obtained in a specified period, e.g., 60 days.) Importantly, anyone failing to comply with the "DBA" statute may not defend or maintain a suit in a court of law, although in such instances it may be possible to delay the suit until the statutory formalities have been observed.

7

CORPORATE PURPOSES AND POWERS

Most corporations operate under a charter granted by a state. Included in that charter is a statement of purpose, written by the incorporators and approved by the state. In addition, corporations operate under state law, which grants them certain powers and restricts them in certain areas.

Corporate Purposes. Under the RMBCA, every corporation has the purpose of engaging in any lawful business, unless a more limited purpose is set forth in the articles. The RMBCA also provides that a corporation engaging in a business that is subject to regulation under another statute (e.g., banking), may incorporate under the RMBCA only if permitted by such other statute.

Many incorporations have found it useful to set forth a statement of purpose that includes a brief description of the activities their corporation will engage in.

For example, a retail store might have purposes similar to the following:

"Purposes: To manufacture, produce, purchase, or otherwise acquire, sell, import, export, distribute, and deal in goods, wares, merchandise and materials of any kind and description."

In addition to this specific list of purposes, there might be a paragraph such as the following, which leaves the door open to other business opportunities:

"The foregoing purposes and activities will be interpreted as examples only and not as limitations, and nothing herein shall be deemed as prohibiting the corporation from extending its activities to any related or otherwise permissible lawful business purposes which may become necessary, profitable, or desirable for the furtherance of the corporate objectives expressed above."

The rationale for the broadly worded purposes clause is that it permits a corporation to take advantage of any opportunity when action must be taken quickly.

Related to the issue of corporate purpose is that of corporate powers. Under the RMBCA, unless the articles provide otherwise, every corporation will have perpetual duration and succession in its corporate name and the same powers as an individual to do all things necessary or convenient to carry out its business and affairs, including without limitation the following powers:

1. To sue and be sued, complain, and defend itself in its corporate name.
2. To have a corporate seal, which may be altered at will.
3. To make and amend bylaws, not inconsistent with its articles of incorporation or with the laws of the state, for managing the business and regulating the affairs of the corporation.
4. To purchase, receive, lease, or otherwise acquire, and own, hold, improve, use, and otherwise deal with, real or personal property, or any legal or equitable interest in property, wherever located.
5. To sell, convey, mortgage, pledge, lease, exchange, and otherwise dispose of all or any part of the property.
6. To purchase, receive, subscribe for, or otherwise

acquire; own, hold, vote, use, sell, mortgage, lend, pledge, or otherwise dispose of; and deal in and with shares or other interests in, or obligations of, any other entity.

7. To make contracts and guarantees, incur liabilities, borrow money, issue its notes, bonds, and other obligations, and secure any of its obligations by mortgage or pledge of any of its property, franchises or income.

8. To lend money, invest, and reinvest its funds, and receive and hold real and personal property as security for repayment.

9. To be a promoter, partner, member, associate, or manager of any partnership, joint venture, trust, or other entity.

10. To conduct its business, locate offices, and exercise the powers granted by law within or without the state.

11. To elect directors and appoint officers, employees, and agents of the corporation, define their duties, fix their compensation, and lend them money and credit.

12. To pay pensions and establish pension plans, pension trusts, profit sharing plans, share bonus plans, share option plans, and benefit or incentive plans for any or all of its current or former directors, officers, employees, and agents.

13. To make donations for the public welfare or for charitable, scientific, or educational purposes.

14. To transact any lawful business that will aid governmental policy.

15. To make payments or donations, or do any other act, not inconsistent with law, that furthers the business and affairs of the corporation.

Beyond these general powers, there are so-called emergency powers. Further, a corporation generally has all powers necessary or convenient to effect any or all of the purposes for which the corporation was formed. This is known as residual power.

Some terminology would be useful here. An *intra vires* act is one within the powers of the corporation. An *ultra vires* contract is one beyond the corporate powers. At common law, where a corporation entered into an ultra vires contract, either the corporation or a third party with whom it contracted could disaffirm the contract since the corporation lacked capacity to enter into the contract. More recently, modern courts have tended to use the doctrine of ratification to validate an otherwise ultra vires contract so long as there is unanimous shareholder approval.

Under the RMBCA, the validity of a corporate act may not be challenged on the ground that the corporation lacked power except in a proceeding by a shareholder against the corporation to enjoin the act, in a proceeding by the corporation through a receiver, trustee, or other legal representative against an incumbent or former director, officer, employee, or agent of the corporation, or in a proceeding by the state attorney general.

Before leaving the subject of corporate powers, three issues are worth addressing. First, older laws did not expressly empower corporations to enter into partnerships. Modern statutes do so; corporations may now serve as partners. Next, since the object of a for-profit enterprise is to conduct business with a view to making a profit, at one point it was unclear whether corporations could make donations for charitable purposes. Today, many statutes explicitly confer upon corporations the power to make donations for such purposes, although this power, like other powers, is subject to an implied limit of reasonableness. Finally, older laws did not expressly confer upon corporations the power to guarantee the debts of others. Modern statutes do so; thus, a corporation can make contracts of suretyship or guaranty, but the power can generally only be exercised in furtherance of the corporate business.

8

FILING THE ARTICLES OF INCORPORATION

Generally, a corporation is organized by the execution and filing of the corporate charter, which is known as the articles of incorporation or, simply, the articles, along with any required filing fees and registry statement. The individuals who form the corporation are known as incorporators. Depending on state law, the incorporators may be required to file a registry statement for informational purposes. Basically, in this document the incorporators set forth the name of the corporation, an address to which correspondence may be directed, the statutory authority under which the business was incorporated, the kinds of businesses to be transacted, and other information as may be required by law.

Among the other duties of the incorporators are signing the articles, delivering them to the secretary of state or other official, and executing the registry statement. A number of states permit one person to serve as incorporator — and/or permit a corporation to serve as the incorporator.

As to what must be contained in the articles, some states have prescribed forms for this purpose, while others allow considerable flexibility. Under the RMBCA, the articles must set forth a corporate name, the number of shares the corporation is authorized to issue, the street address of the initial registered office, the name of the registered agent to accept service of process, and the name and address of each incorporator. Under the RMBCA, the articles may also set forth the following:

1. The names and addresses of the individuals who are to serve as the initial directors
2. Provisions not inconsistent with law regarding:
   a. the purpose or purposes for which the corporation is organized
   b. managing the business and regulating the affairs of the corporation
   c. defining, limiting, and regulating the powers of the corporation, its board of directors, and shareholders
   d. a par value for authorized shares or classes of shares
   e. the imposition of personal liability on shareholders for debts of the corporation to a specified extent and upon specified conditions
3. Any provision required by law or permitted to be set forth in the bylaws.

The articles may cover many other points as well, such as establishing preemptive rights and transfer restrictions, allowing for cumulative voting, and calling for special meetings. If all the documents are in order, the secretary of state will approve the articles, file the original, and return a certified copy of the articles and a receipt to the incorporators. (In some states, the secretary may just mark the copies to show the articles have been filed and endorsed with the required approval.) It may be necessary to make sure that a certified copy of the articles is recorded in the office of the clerk of the county in which the corporation will do business, own real estate, or maintain its principal office. Some states and localities have additional requirements.

Note that the secretary of state merely reviews the incorporation documents to determine if they comply with the filing requirements of the state. The secretary of state's office does not review the documents for such matters as corporate governance and capitalization, compliance with other business or regulatory laws, or tax status. Thus, in certain instances where the wording of one or more provisions is important, an attorney should be consulted to ensure that the articles are drawn properly. For example, in order for a nonprofit corporation to qualify as such for federal tax purposes, the corporate purposes and other sections must conform with federal tax laws.

Unless a delayed effective date is specified, the corporate existence generally begins when the articles are filed. Under the RMBCA, the secretary of state's filing of the articles is conclusive proof that the incorporators satisfied all conditions precedent to incorporation, except in a proceeding by the state to cancel or revoke the incorporation or to involuntarily dissolve the corporation.

After the articles are filed, the incorporators or the board of directors named in the articles hold a meeting to complete the corporate organization. Subject to state law, such a meeting may be held within or outside of the state. This meeting is held in the same manner as other meetings of stockholders or directors. (See Key 15, CORPORATE MEETINGS.) In setting up the articles, incorporators may specify procedures for voting, such as a supermajority for the adoption of important measures. It is not a good idea to require a unanimous vote, even on the most important issues, since that can be difficult to achieve. In such instances it might be preferable to require the unanimous vote of the quorum present.

At the initial meeting, the articles are ordered into the record of the meeting and the bylaws are adopted, or a committee is appointed to draft them. Under the RMBCA, the bylaws may contain any provision for managing the business and regulating the affairs of the corporation that is not inconsistent with state law. If any restrictions on the power of the directors are set forth in the articles, third parties are bound by them. Restrictions that are only in the bylaws, however, are not binding, since the bylaws are not filed and made a public record.

9

TAX ASPECTS
OF FORMING
A CORPORATION

When a taxpayer transfers property in exchange for other property, there is normally a gain or a loss. Such gain or loss is computed by comparing the adjusted basis, or cost, of the property given up with the value of the property received. This realized gain or loss must be recognized for tax purposes unless a particular exception applies.

Under Section 351 of the tax law, if one or more persons transfer property to a corporation solely in exchange for stock or securities, and the transferors, taken as a group, are in control of the corporation immediately after the exchange, the transferors will not recognize gain or loss in the exchange. Thus, in the normal course of events, owners of a business who decide to incorporate will not have to pay any income tax based on the transaction. The theory is that such transfers represent mere changes in form and thus should not be recognized until an economically significant event occurs. The same principle applies not only to transfers to new corporations but to existing corporations as well.

Section 351 is very important for closely held corporations, most of which should be eligible for the benefits of this provision. Note, however, that all such shareholders are required to file a statement with their federal income tax returns providing details as to the tax-deferred exchange. In effect, Section 351 is a deferral provision. Thus, it merely postpones the day that the realized gain or loss will be recognized. One might ask why one might ever opt out of Section 351. If, however, a transferor has a realized loss that he wishes to recognize or desires to take a stepped-up basis in assets transferred, he or she might decide on a taxable incorporation. This can be accomplished either by a sale to the corporation — a sale of assets for cash — or the failure to meet one of the requirements of Section 351, such as the control test, as spelled out below.

For the purposes defined in Section 351, a *person* includes not only individuals, but estates, trusts, partnerships, associations, companies, and corporations. The term *property* includes not only money, realty, personal property, and intangibles, but also such items as patents and patentable know-how. Thus, secret processes and formulas, along with proprietary information in the general nature of patentable inventory, qualify as property under Section 351. However, property does not encompass services — whether past, present, or future — so the distinction between past services and know-how, which is property for tax purposes, is important. Further, transferors of services who also transfer property to the corporation in exchange for stock or other securities, will include the securities received for services in determining whether the control requirement (described below) is satisfied. Since the law seeks to prevent nominal transfers by existing stockholders in order to qualify someone else's exchange as tax-free, the transferred property must not be of relatively small value compared to the stock already owned or to be received in exchange for services. As a rule of thumb, the IRS generally will not consider property to be of relatively small value if the fair market value of the property transferred equals at least 10% of the fair market value of the stock or securities already owned by the transferor or to be received in exchange for services by the transferor.

Stock includes all shares — be they voting or nonvoting, common or preferred — but excludes stock rights and warrants; securities refers to all debt with the exception of short-term notes. The reason is that the nonrecognition sections — including Section 351 — are designed to permit the tax-free transfer of property only if the transfer is not analogous to a sale. The problem with short-term notes is their close resemblance to cash as distinct from an ongoing interest in the corporation. Although what constitutes a short-term note is not free from doubt, generally, notes with terms of five years or less will not qualify as securities.

While on the subject of debt securities, it is worth mentioning that the market-discount rules added by the Tax Reform Act of 1984 may cause a shareholder who receives debt from a new corporation to have market-discount income, which is reportable as ordinary income.

The Control Test. It was noted earlier that for Section 351 to apply, the transferors must be in control of the corporation immediately after the exchange. The control test is taken from the reorganization area of the Internal Revenue Code. For this purpose, control means ownership of at least 80% of the total combined voting power of all classes of stock entitled to vote and ownership of at least 80% of the total number of shares of all other classes of stock. Note that if two or more classes of voting stock are issued, the transferors must take back shares possessing 80% or more of the *total* voting power, regardless of the number of shares in each class. However, if two or more classes of nonvoting stock are issued, the transferors must receive at least 80% of the number of shares in each class of nonvoting stock.

The test for control requirement is the interest that the transferors *as a group* receive in the corporation. Thus, if Thatcher and Hatcher each transfer property for 50% of the shares of the business, the control requirement would be satisfied even though neither person individually winds up with the required control. Note, however, that the stock ownership must be actual, since the attribution-of-ownership rules do not apply here. Thus, if husband, wife, and son each own a third of the shares of a corporation and only husband and son transfer property to the corporation in exchange for securities, the transaction will not qualify under Section 351 because the transferors (husband and son) will not be 80% in "control" immediately after the exchange.

As to what "immediately after the exchange" means, this does not require an instantaneous transfer, so that if control is achieved as a result of a series of planned transactions, the requirements would be met. Thus, if the rights of the parties have been defined prior to the exchange and the execution of the plan follows ordinary procedure, the exchange should qualify as being tax-free. Note that a formalized agreement among the parties is not normally required — just a general plan among the parties that contemplates the transfer by several persons of specified cash and other property so as to unite the transferors into the requisite group.

A recurring issue in the Section 351 area concerns the receipt of so-called "boot." If a transferor receives not only stock or securities in the swap but some other property or cash "to boot," any gain is recognized but only to the extent of the fair market value of the boot received. Losses are still not recognized. If the transferee (i.e., the corporation) assumes the transferor's debt, the assumption — or taking subject to — is generally not treated as money paid to the transferor.

Assuming that a transferor transfers property in exchange for stock or securities under Section 351, the transferor's basis in the stock and securities received is generally the same as the basis in the property given up. Such basis is decreased by the sum of any boot received as well as the transferor's debt the corporation assumes or takes subject to, and increased by any gain recognized in the exchange. The stock is a capital asset in the hands of the transferor even if the assets transferred were not.

Let's take an example. If Thatcher transfers property with a fair market value of $100 and a basis to her of $40 in a

Section 351 exchange, her basis in the stock and securities received would still be $40. However, if Thatcher receives stock with a fair market value of $70 and $30 in boot, she would recognize gain of $30, and her basis in the stock would be $40. Note that a transferor who takes more than one class of stock and securities must allocate his or her basis among them according to their relative fair market values.

So much for the transferor. The corporation's basis in the assets it receives is the same as their basis in the hands of the transferor, increased by any gain the transferor-shareholder recognized in the exchange. This carryover of basis applies to each item of property so that no reallocation is necessary among the property received by the corporation unless gain has been recognized by the transferor. Note that the tax status of these assets to the corporation — as capital assets, depreciable business property, etc. — depends on how they are used by the corporation, irrespective of the status they had with the transferor, but the corporation's holding period includes the transferor's holding period.

There are a number of other issues associated with corporate formation. For example, professional or service corporations frequently have substantial accounts receivable, etc. Generally, on formation of the new corporation, accounts receivable and payable will be transferred to the corporation. If the proprietorship or partnership was on the cash basis method of accounting, charging off specific accounts receivable as they became worthless rather than setting up a bad debt reserve, and deducting business expenses as they accrued, no particular tax problem would ordinarily arise. However, if the business employed an accrual method with a reserve for bad debts, this poses potential tax problems that should be explored with an accountant or other tax adviser.

See also 28/CORPORATE TAXATION and 29/TWO SPECIAL TAX PROBLEMS.

10

DE FACTO AND DE JURE CORPORATIONS

After the articles of incorporation have been filed and any required fees paid, a question may arise as to when corporate existence begins. This, too, varies according to state law. Under Florida law, for instance, commencement of corporate existence, if specified in the articles, may occur up to five days before or 90 days after filing. Under the RMBCA, unless a delayed effective date is specified, corporate existence begins when the articles are filed. The RMBCA also provides that filing with the secretary of state is conclusive proof that the incorporators have satisfied all of the conditions for incorporation.

De Jure Corporations. Sometimes the state may move to cancel or revoke the incorporation or to dissolve the corporation. If there is a defect in the incorporation process, the question arises as to whether the corporate identity is to be respected. If there is at least substantial compliance with the state's laws, the corporation will be deemed to have *de jure* status. In this case, the corporation may not be attacked by the state or by a third party (such as a creditor trying to reach a shareholder directly). Note that perfect compliance with state law is not necessary, just substantial compliance. Thus, there ordinarily must be compliance with all mandatory provisions of the law in order to qualify for *de jure* status. Words like "must" tend to indicate a mandatory provision, while words like "may" tend to evidence what is called a directory provision.

De Facto Corporations. In some cases there may have been a "colorable attempt in good faith" to organize a corporation pursuant to law, but some defect in the incorporation process has prevented classification as a *de jure* corporation. If the corporation has exercised corporate powers such as issuing stock or electing directors, it should have the same status as a *de jure* corporation to enter into contracts. Such a corporation is called a *de facto* corporation, and only the state through the attorney general's office may attack its validity. The procedure used by the state for this purpose is called a quo warranto proceeding, in which the state essentially asks, "By what warrant or authority does the corporation exist?"

In effect, a *de facto* corporation is treated as a valid corporation with respect to third parties. Thus, it is important to understand the elements of the *de facto* doctrine. Although what constitutes a "colorable attempt" at compliance is not totally clear, it generally involves an effort to prepare and file the articles. As to what constitutes "in good faith," it generally means that the shareholders raising the defense of *de facto* status were not aware of the organizational defects when they ran the business.

Other Alternatives. Should the organizational procedures not give rise to either a *de jure* or a *de facto* corporation — for example, if no powers were ever exercised by the corporation — even third parties may attack its existence. In such cases, the shareholders may be held individually liable, although even here courts have split on the question of whether all shareholders should be held responsible or just those who actively participated in the management of the business.

11

LIMITED LIABILITY

As noted previously, the seminal advantage of the corporate form is the limited liability it offers the shareholders. The basic premise is that corporate creditors are not permitted to satisfy corporate debts by suing or otherwise going against the shareholders. In fact, if the owners are personally liable for all the debts of the business, the entity is not a corporation.

When an existing business is incorporated, the former owners of the business continue to be liable to creditors of the old business for taxes and debts incurred prior to incorporation unless the owners have been released from this liability. In the case of incorporation of a partnership, subject to state law, the former partners may be held liable for debts incurred after incorporation if it is determined that the creditor was not notified of the dissolution of the partnership.

Sole proprietors and general partners have unlimited personal liability in all obligations of the business. However, it is useful to compare the status of a limited partner in a limited partnership with the liability of a corporate shareholder. The liability of a limited partner is limited to the amount of his capital contribution unless he takes part in the management of the business, in which case he may assume personal liability. On the other hand, the shareholder of a corporation may participate fully in the operations of the business without incurring personal liability for the debts and obligations of the business. As a practical matter, though, for a new enterprise, banks and some other lenders may require personal guarantees from the shareholders as a means of ensuring payment. However, certain creditors such as trade creditors do not typically require such assurances so long as the business is a going concern and there is no marked impairment of credit.

Another recurring question is whether insolvency of the corporation will absolve the owners of tax obligations, especially for employment tax. Classically, a troubled corporation has creditors who are pressing it for payment. Meanwhile, it holds employment taxes that it is obligated to pay over to the government. The federal tax code levies a significant penalty against corporate officers and other "responsible persons" for failure to withhold and pay over such taxes and the government will go after such individuals personally. "Responsible persons" are defined as those who have the duty to perform or the power to direct the act of collecting, accounting for, or paying over trust fund moneys. At issue then is which party was under a duty to see to it that taxes were withheld, collected, or paid over to the government as of the specific time the failure to withhold, to collect, or pay over the taxes occurred. Of course, such failure must be "willful," which basically means intentional, deliberate, voluntary, and knowing, as distinguished from accidental. In any case, it is important not to use such earmarked funds for other purposes.

The basic question in this area is whether or not directors can be found liable for their actions, thus negating limited liability. For instance, if the board of directors declares an illegal dividend, the directors will be jointly and severally liable to the corporation for the benefit of creditors or preferred shareholders who were affected by the dividend. In states that follow the original MBCA, the corporation can collect the full amount of this "illegal" dividend. Many jurisdictions, however, limit recovery to the amount of the injury suffered, which is basically the amount owed to the creditors and the amount by which the illegal dividend impaired preferences of the preferred shares. Further, modern statutes tend to protect directors from liability when they relied in good faith on the books of the corporation.

It should be noted that shareholders as well as directors may be personally liable for illegal dividends. Generally, in insolvent corporations, each shareholder who received a dividend will be required to return it to the corporation for the benefit of creditors and the preferred shareholders. Shareholders in solvent corporations are generally permitted to keep an illegal distribution, assuming that they received it in good faith (i.e., they did not know that the dividend came from an improper source.) Of course, if the shareholder knew of the illegal source of the dividends, or can be charged with such knowledge, a different result may ensue.

12

"PIERCING THE CORPORATE VEIL"

Even if a corporation has been properly formed, it may be operated in such a manner as to lose the advantages of incorporation. The phrase "piercing the corporate veil" is legal jargon referring to court action that has the effect of ignoring the existence of a corporation separate and distinct from its owners. Generally, the action involves a lawsuit by a creditor against the shareholders where the organization has been thinly capitalized (i.e., underfinanced) or where corporate shareholders have been using the corporate form as an alter ego (the legal phrase is "excessive domination").

The shareholders may be liable if it appears the corporation was organized and operated without adequate capital to meet the obligations that could reasonably be expected to arise. The shareholders may also be liable if they have not treated the corporation as a separate entity but really as a kind of alter ego of themselves. This is most likely to occur in closely held corporations. Classically, this arises where the shareholders have failed to distinguish between the corporation's affairs and the assets of the owners (known as commingling) or where corporate procedures have not been observed (e.g., failure to hold shareholders' and directors' meetings, failure to keep separate books of accounts for the corporation, failure actually to issue stock, etc.). Note that neither of these theories of liability requires a fraud on third parties. Of course, courts may ignore the corporate form where it has been used to evade a statutory or contractual obligation.

Although cases of piercing the corporate veil are relatively rare, owners of closely held corporations would be well advised to consider the following guidelines:

1. The corporation should be adequately capitalized to meet its obligations.
2. The shareholders should not treat corporate property as if it belonged to them.
3. The separateness of the corporate form should be emphasized in the day-to-day operation of the business, so that, for example, corporate transactions should be reflected on corporate and not personal stationery, and payments should be made out of corporate and not personal accounts. No representation should be made leading others to believe that the entity is being operated on some other basis, such as a partnership (e.g., referring to a fellow shareholder as "my partner").
4. The formalities of corporate procedure (e.g., maintaining minutes of meetings) should be strictly observed. This can have tax as well as nontax consequences. If, during the course of an audit, the agent asks to see what minutes support a bonus declared to a key shareholder, the importance of having observed such formalities will be quickly appreciated.

Importantly with respect to small businesses, if a corporation becomes insolvent, debts owed by the corporation to the shareholders may be subordinated to the claims of other creditors, so that the shareholders' claims will not be paid until all other creditors have been paid. This is the case even where a shareholder's claims have been "fully secured." Typically this will arise when there has been corporate mismanagement, thin capitalization, or bad faith by the shareholder toward other creditors of the corporation.

13

PROMOTERS

The word *promoter* does not have quite the same meaning in the law of incorporation as it does in everyday usage. In law, a promoter is understood to be one who causes a corporation to be formed, organized, and financed. The promoter(s) may be a law firm engaged for this specific purpose, the owners of the proposed corporation, or someone else. (Note: an incorporator is not necessarily a promoter but is merely someone who signs the articles.)

The promoter cannot act as an agent for a corporation-to-be because that corporation does not yet exist. Thus, any contract signed by a promoter before the official existence of the corporation begins cannot be construed to be the corporation's contract or obligation. Of course, the corporation can become liable on the contract simply by adopting it. This involves the corporation's taking some affirmative act — by express words or otherwise — to adopt the contract. Or the adoption may be implied from the corporation's acceptance of the benefits of the contract with full knowledge of the contract's existence.

Novation. If a promoter contracts with a third party for the benefit of a corporation to be formed, and if the corporation does not subsequently adopt the contract, the promoter will still be bound on the contract unless there is a novation. Under contract law, a novation occurs where a new contract substitutes a new party to receive benefits and to assume duties under the terms of the old contract. As an example, assume that Smith contracts to sell his home to Johnson. Before the closing date, Smith, Johnson, and Kelly execute a new agreement under which all rights and duties in connection with the transaction are transferred from Johnson to Kelly. The old Smith-Johnson contract is discharged by novation. In the context of incorporation, if a corporation adopts a preincorporation contract executed by a promoter, and if the third party agrees to accept the corporation as the debtor, there is a novation by which the corporation is substituted for the promoter.

Stock Subscriptions. There are numerous types of preincorporation agreements, including contracts for tax advice and underwriting expenses, but the classic preincorporation agreement involves the securing of subscriptions (commitments) to buy a stated number of unissued shares. If the subscription is in proper written form, signed by the subscriber(s), it is irrevocable and thus enforceable by the corporation after formation. If a subscriber defaults in payment, the corporation may collect the amount owed, or, unless the agreement provides otherwise, it may rescind the agreement and sell the shares to someone else.

What is the promoter's liability if the corporation rejects the preincorporation contracts or does not do as was agreed — or never comes into existence at all? Can the other party hold the promoter liable? The answer basically comes down to whether the promoter has clearly specified that he is acting in the name of the proposed corporation and not individually. If so, the other party must rely on the credit standing of the proposed corporation and cannot act against the promoter individually. If not, the promoter may be held personally liable on preincorporation contracts.

14

BOARD OF DIRECTORS

As stated previously, the authority to manage the affairs of the corporation is vested in the board of directors. Provisions governing the actions of the board are set in the articles of incorporation. The board itself adopts the bylaws.

The directors set the business tone and policy and select the principal officers of the business. The directors have the right to inspect corporate books and records and properties. Generally, directors are not entitled to compensation for their services as directors unless such services are extraordinary or compensation is provided for in the articles or in a board resolution before the services are actually rendered. Note that directors are not agents of the shareholders who have elected them. Directors are fiduciaries owing their duties principally to the corporation. Their powers are derived from the state, not delegated by the stockholders.

The list of powers given to the board of directors in the RMBCA is so broad that it reduces the likelihood that an act would be found to be beyond the board's powers. In fact, even if a quorum of the company's directors cannot be assembled because of a catastrophic event, the RMBCA allows for emergency powers. In an emergency situation, the board may modify lines of succession to accommodate the incapacity of any director, officer, employee or agent, may relocate the corporation's principal office, may designate alternative principal offices or regional offices, or may authorize the officers to do so. The board members may set the size of the board either expressly or because the number of directors is fixed in the bylaws and the board is empowered to amend the bylaws. To prevent direct manipulation of the board, however, the RMBCA provides for shareholder approval of increases or decreases in the size of the board of 30% or more.

In some cases, state law may permit the directors to act via conference telephone or similar communication equipment without meeting face to face. Directors may also act by unanimous written consent without a meeting, unless restricted by the articles or bylaws. Generally, there is no statutory provision allowing directors to act by proxy, however, thus making it clear that directors are obligated to assume responsibility for making corporate decisions.

Although the authority to manage the corporation's affairs is vested in the directors as a body, often, the board will appoint committees of its own members to act for the board in certain types of matters (e.g., an audit committee). Further, many statutes authorize the creation of an executive committee, which exercises the authority of the full board subject to certain limits. For instance, the RMBCA provides that the executive committee may not authorize dividend or other distributions, fill vacancies on the board, or adopt, amend, or repeal the bylaws.

In the classic management structure, the majority shareholders elect all of the directors. If the articles include provision for cumulative voting rights or contractual rights for the minority shareholders, then the voting procedures are somewhat different, as discussed in Key 15, CORPORATE MEETINGS. Stockholders do not elect the president and other officers of the corporation. This is the prerogative of the board, which generally entrusts day-to-day management of the business to these officers. Minor officers may be appointed by the board or by the president. All officers serve at the pleasure of the board, although of course there may be a contract for services for a specified time period. Some courts have held that a contract with an officer beyond the board's term is void. A long-term contract is more likely to be upheld if of a duration of five years or less and if, expressly or impliedly, the directors have reserved the power to dismiss the individual for incompetence or gross abuse of position without being liable for breach of contract.

Especially in a small corporation, the same persons may serve as officers and directors and may hold more than one office, except that some state laws may prohibit the same individual from serving both as president and secretary. Persons holding more than one office should not sign corporate documents in such dual—or multiple—capacity.

Note that officers and employees are viewed as agents. This means that the corporation will generally not be bound by an agreement entered into by someone who lacked the authority to execute it. Basically, there are three kinds of authority. First, actual authority may be expressly conferred by the corporate bylaws or resolutions; in addition, an agent has implied authority to do what can be reasonably implied from a grant of express authority. Second, there is authority that the corporation allows third parties to reasonably believe the agent possesses ("apparent authority"). Third, there is authority by virtue of one's position in the corporation. This "power of position" is actually a special case of apparent authority. Even if an officer lacks de jure authority, if he exercises some authority of a corporate office, under color of title of such office, he may be deemed a de facto officer.

When a vacancy on the board occurs, the remaining directors may elect a new board member. The RMBCA also gives this authority to shareholders unless the articles of incorporation provide otherwise. Note that persons exercising the functions of directors under some color of office, despite their lack of proper qualifications, election, or other requirements necessary for de jure directors, or despite even their removal, may still bind the corporation as de facto directors. Further, anyone assuming to act as a director is subject to the duties of a director.

A vacancy may occur in a number of ways. First, a director may resign at any time by delivering written notice to the board, its chairman, or to the corporation itself. The resignation is effective when the notice is delivered, unless the notice specifies a later date. Second, directors may be removed by a judicial proceeding upon a finding that the director engaged in fraudulent or dishonest conduct or gross abuse of authority or discretion. The court must find that such removal is in the best interests of the corporation. Third, the shareholders may remove the director with or without cause, unless the articles provide the directors may be removed only for cause. Where cumulative voting is authorized, special rules apply to the removal of directors. Note that some affirmative expression of assent to serve as a director is required. Thus, the courts will not impose the duties and liabilities of a director unless the individual assumes the functions of a director. A director elected to fill a vacancy must stand for election at the next annual meeting of shareholders even if the term otherwise would continue beyond the meeting. Some jurisdictions follow earlier versions of the MBCA and provide that directors elected to fill a vacancy remain in office for the term of their predecessor.

In some cases, an agreement may be entered into among the directors or between a director and a shareholder, committing the directors to vote in a particular manner. At common law, such a contract was invalid since the corporation is entitled to the unfettered discretion of the board. However, if a close corporation is involved and the agreement involves specified narrow areas such as the declaration of dividends or the selection of officers, it might be permitted. Thus, if a company had three shareholders who agree among themselves as directors that they will distribute 40% of the profits to the shareholders as dividends, the agreement is probably sufficiently narrow as to be acceptable.

15

CORPORATE MEETINGS

Under the RMBCA, following the formation of a corporation, there is an organizational meeting. If the initial directors have been named in the articles of incorporation, those directors meet to appoint officers, adopt bylaws, and carry on any other business brought before the meeting. If initial directors have not been named in the articles, the incorporator(s) hold an organizational meeting to elect a board of directors.

The RMBCA makes it clear that action required to be taken by incorporators at an organizational meeting may be taken without a meeting if the action taken is supported by one or more written consents describing the action taken and signed by each incorporator. In any case, the incorporators or the board of directors adopt the initial bylaws, which are the rules for the internal government of the corporation.

After the corporation has been organized there are two kinds of shareholder meetings—annual and special. For annual meetings the bylaws generally fix the date. Although the most important function is to elect the directors, the agenda may include reports from management, consideration of resolutions introduced on behalf of management, and such other matters as may properly come before such meetings. The notice of the meetings will usually set forth the purposes. Special meetings are held between the annual meetings and may be called pursuant to state law, the articles, or the bylaws. The business conducted at the meeting must be confined to the purposes set forth in the notice. Hence, shareholders are entitled to receive notice of, and to be represented in person or by proxy at, the meetings. A notice should not only identify the place, day, and hour of the meeting but also, in case of special meetings, the purpose for which the meeting is being called. Notice may be waived before or after a meeting and in some cases by participation of shareholders without objection to lack of notice.

In order to provide the proper notice there must be a voting list. State laws generally require a corporation to keep at its principal place of business or at the office of its transfer agent or registrar, a shareholder list, giving names and addresses of all shareholders and the number and class of shares held by each. This list is a record open to reasonable shareholder inspection. Such a list is especially important if there must be a court hearing to compel (or enjoin the holding of) a meeting. For this purpose, a writ of *mandamus* or injunction is the traditional legal remedy.

Whether the meeting is annual or special, a quorum is required in order to start the meeting officially. (Courts are split as to whether a meeting that begins with a quorum may continue after some shareholders walk out so that less than a quorum is present.) Unless otherwise specified in the articles of incorporation a majority of the shares entitled to vote constitutes a quorum in most states.

Voting. Shareholders generally are entitled to one vote for each share of stock they own. Most matters are decided on the basis of majority rule. Some variations may be specified in the articles of incorporation or the bylaws. The election of directors, for instance, can be decided either by straight voting — one vote per share for each directorship open, in which case the majority shareholders would elect all the directors — or by cumulative voting, so that shareholders could vote all their shares for one director, in which case there is a better chance for minority representation on the board. Other variable requirements include that for a supermajority (in which a high percentage — say, 80% — of the stockholders must vote in favor of an action) or a superquorum, in which more than a simple majority of the shareholders must attend in order for there to be a quorum.

A few courts and state laws have not looked favorably on such super requirements, finding them overly restrictive to the rights of the majority. For example, with a superquorum, a shareholder could deliberately remain absent, thus preventing a quorum at a meeting intended to vote on matters to which he or she was opposed. Some early court decisions did strike down such arrangements, but more recent decisions have tended to uphold them, as necessary to meet the special needs of the close corporation.

As has been noted, supermajority requirements may lead to deadlocks since they can allow a minority shareholder to block proposed corporate action. In cases where the election of new directors is blocked, the bylaws could provide that the directors will continue in office until their successors are elected. Other shareholder agreements provide for a dispute-resolution mechanism. This allows the shareholders themselves to devise standard procedures for resolution *before* a dispute actually arises — at which time each side would otherwise press for a procedure favorable to its own interests. Further, different classes of stock can be set up to keep voting control of the corporation within a family or funding group (see Key 20/ISSUANCE OF STOCK). However, only if the share certificates contain a conspicuous notation as to its "close" status and the presence of shareholder agreements will any transferee of shares covered by the agreement or special provision in the articles be bound.

Meeting Format. The general format of a shareholders' meeting includes a secretary's report, treasurer's report, election of directors, old business, and new business. The format of a board of directors meeting is similar, except that here the elections are for company officers. Meetings of the directors are held at least annually and sometimes more frequently, depending on the size and complexity of the business, for it is the directors who are legally responsible for the running of the corporation. They may delegate powers to the top officers, who are often themselves directors, but it is the board that holds the ultimate authority to manage the corporation's affairs.

Valid action can occur only if the directors act as a body at a validly convened meeting and not through individual deliberations. Directors vote per capita and generally may not vote by proxy. A validly convened meeting is one with the proper notice and a quorum present. A majority of those present thus has power to decide any issues that come before the meeting.

16

PROFESSIONAL SERVICE CORPORATIONS

There are a number of reasons why professionals should consider incorporation. Although the IRS now respects the existence of the incorporated professional, the battle was not an easy one. In 1954, the U.S. Court of Appeals for the Ninth Circuit held in the famous Kintner decision, 216 F.2d 418, that a common law association of doctors, which ran a clinic, would be taxable as a corporation and thus could legally maintain a tax-qualified pension plan for its members. The initial response of the IRS was not to follow the Kintner decision, but subsequently it agreed to do so.

Under the so-called Kintner regulations, an association was defined as an unincorporated firm that directed a continuing enterprise for profit and that had a majority of the following corporate features: continuity of life, centralization of management, free transferability of interests, and limited liability. State law was to be followed as to whether an entity met the foregoing characteristics. Such regulations effectively made it impossible for a proprietorship or partnership to realize corporate treatment, but they left the door open for state legislatures to enact laws that permit professionals to realize the advantages of incorporation. They did so. Currently, if a professional corporation or association is valid under state law, it will be respected as such for federal tax purposes.

Generally, the professional corporation law is a supplement to the state's business corporation act, which is also applicable to professional corporations except where in case of conflict. As the professional corporation laws vary among the states, they must be studied carefully before incorporation is to be undertaken.

Under these laws, only persons licensed to practice the particular profession can own an interest in the corporation. For example, upon the death of a licensed dentist who held an interest in a professional corporation or association, the estate would have to sell his interest to the business itself or to another licensed dentist. Some states provide for an immediate redemption or other sale of the deceased's stock; others provide for the disposition of stock within a limited time (e.g., 90 days). Some states actually establish the price for the shares (or a formula for determining the price); others require that the articles or bylaws provide for the purchase or redemption of the shares upon the death of the shareholder. Some states provide that, absent a provision in the articles, bylaws, or an agreement, the corporation must purchase the shares owed by the deceased.

Importantly, an incorporated professional will not be personally liable for the negligent acts of his associates, as is the case with a partnership. In fact, a professional in a partnership may be liable even if he did not participate in the transaction out of which the liability arose. Incorporated professionals remain liable to clients or patients for their own negligence and, perhaps, for the negligence of anyone under their supervision and control. This represents a broader liability than exists in ordinary corporations but a narrower liability than would result in a professional partnership.

Other aspects of these laws generally require that shareholders in the corporation practice the same profession and, typically, even the same specialty. The minimum number of incorporators is commonly one, but some states require two (or even three). As regards the number of directors and officers required, many states allow a solo practitioner to serve as sole director and hold all of the corporate offices.

Practitioners who incorporate must comply with the usual requirements: filing the articles, paying the required fees, adopting the bylaws at the required meeting, filing the annual reports, holding stockholder meetings, keeping minutes, and satisfying other indicia of corporateness. Like the sole shareholder of a closely held corporation, the incorporated practitioner must treat the corporation as such, or else the corporate identity will not be respected. It is crucial that the shareholders deal with the outside world in their business and not their personal capacities (e.g., using a corporate and not a personal bank account to pay corporate expenses). The corporation should file all annual reports required by law, and any indebtedness incurred should be in the name of the corporation. If shareholders are required to guarantee any notes personally, it should be made clear that they are acting as guarantors and not as principals on the debt. Insurance policies should be issued (or reissued) in the name of the new corporation, taxes should be paid by the corporation, assets should be held in the corporate name, and the corporation should be billed for all purchases made.

The corporation should request an employer identification number from the IRS and refer to itself for all purposes in its corporate name followed by the appropriate designation (P.C. or P.A.). Not only should the books of the corporation be separate from the books of the individual practitioner(s), but no records should be maintained that imply that any particular clients or patients are being serviced by a given shareholder. Thus, billing of clients or patients should be done only in the name of the corporation.

17

DUTIES OF OFFICERS AND DIRECTORS

Directors and officers alike owe fiduciary duties of care and loyalty to the corporation and to the shareholders. That is, they are required to act in the best interests of the corporation with "undivided and unselfish" loyalty and to use that degree of care in the management of the business that ordinary and prudent people would use in similar circumstances in the handling of their own affairs. Although the following description will emphasize the role of the directors, the same general principles apply to the officers, although the scope of an officer's obligations will be determined partly by the position he or she occupies. (In the rest of this key we will use only the male pronoun as a stylistic convenience.)

Under the RMBCA, a director must discharge his duties as a director, including his duties as a member of a committee: (1) in good faith; (2) with the care an ordinarily prudent person in a like position would exercise under similar circumstances; and (3) in a manner he reasonably believes to be in the best interests of the corporation.

The RMBCA goes on to provide that a director is entitled to rely on information, opinions, reports, or statements, including financial statements and other financial data, if prepared or presented by:

(1) one or more officers or employees of the corporation whom the director reasonably believes to be reliable and competent in the matter presented;

(2) legal counsel, public accountants, or other persons as to matters the director reasonably believes merit confidence;

(3) a committee of the board of directors of which he is not a member, if the director reasonably believes the committee merits confidence.

A director who fails to measure up to the required level of care in discharging his duties and thereby injures the corporation will be liable to the corporation for damages caused. In these cases the "business judgment" rule is commonly invoked. This rule is that a director will not be held responsible so long as his acts were taken in the exercise of informed business judgment. As an example, the acceptance of a note for a judgment, rather than enforcing it for execution, has been held to fall within the rule. However, a director will not be acting in good faith if he has knowledge concerning a matter that makes reliance on business judgment otherwise permitted by law unwarranted. Clearly, a director may not invoke the rule if he causes the corporation to engage in acts that are illegal or contrary to public policy.

Some directors defend themselves in such actions by stating that they only served gratuitously or as figureheads. Such defenses have generally been rejected by the courts. Similarly, old age, bad health, and other disabilities have been held not to constitute good defenses, although some courts have applied these factors in reaching a decision.

Conflict of Interest. The other requirement that directors act in good faith is often referred to as the duty of loyalty to serve the broad interests of the corporation. The director thus may not serve his own interests at the expense of the corporation. The problem may arise where a director contracts with his corporation or where the corporation contracts with another entity in which one of its directors or officers is directly or indirectly involved. At common law, a director's interest in a contract with his corporation made the contract voidable at the option of that corporation without regard to fairness. Today, in many states, a corporation's contract with an interested director will not be voidable solely because of the director's interest if the contract is fair and reasonable to the corporation or if all material facts, including the director's interest, are disclosed to the shareholders.

The RMBCA deals with the conflict-of-interest problem by providing that such a transaction will not be voidable by the corporation solely by reason of the director's interest in the transaction if any of the following is true:

1. The material facts of the transaction and the director's interest were disclosed or known to the board of directors or a committee of the board and the board or committee authorized, approved, or ratified the transaction;

2. The material facts of the transaction and the director's interest were disclosed or known to the shareholders entitled to vote and they authorized, approved, or ratified the transaction;

3. The transaction was fair to the corporation.

The conflict-of-interest problem can arise in closely held corporations. For instance, a director may obtain an interest in a business competing with the corporation, or a director may purchase a claim, debt, or obligation owed to the corporation. The duty of loyalty bars all directors from taking for themselves any advantage or business opportunity that properly belongs to the corporation; each director owes the corporation a right of first refusal, which means a right to acquire the opportunity on the same terms as were offered to the director.

Another conflict-of-interest problem can arise in regard to compensation for services rendered. Thus, a dissident minority shareholder might file suit alleging that excessive compensation was paid to a director, with resultant harm to the corporation. Although directors are not ordinarily entitled to compensation for performing the usual and customary duties of their office, the board is empowered to fix the compensation of directors unless otherwise provided. The board is also empowered to fix salaries of others for services actually rendered. The point is that any payment over and above reasonable compensation may be attacked as wasteful.

Indemnification. The fact that liability may ensue in so many different contexts means that eligibility for indemnification from the corporation can be extremely important. State statutes vary, and much depends on whether the defendant prevails in the case. Generally, if a director — or officer — is accused of wrongdoing and wins, state law will permit the corporation to reimburse him for litigation expenses. If the defendant settles the case or loses, however, a different result may apply. This is why laws in many states permit a corporation to carry insurance to protect the corporation against liability to directors and officers for indemnification and to protect the officials involved against any liability arising out of their service to the business. Regardless of whether state law specifically authorizes the purchase of such a "D & O" (directors and officers) policy, the power to do so is probably implied in the corporate power to provide executive compensation.

Overall, the business-judgment rule will insulate managers for mistakes of judgment arrived at in good faith. Directors and officers alike owe a fiduciary duty to act in good faith and in the best interest of the corporation. Directors may be held liable for improper dividends and distributions just as officers may be held responsible for an improper denial of access to corporate books and records. It is worth noting that officers and agents are generally liable for any acts committed even if such actions are within the scope of their employment. Moreover, the corporation would be liable under the agency doctrine of respondeat superior. An officer could be held personally liable on a contract if it is shown that the officer was the "alter ego" of the corporation or if the officer signed as an individual rather than as an agent for the corporation.

18

"FOREIGN" (OUT-OF-STATE) BUSINESS

No matter how small or how large a corporation, it is incorporated in only one state. This is its home state, its legal domicile, regardless of where its principal offices are located. For example, the Ford Motor Company (like many other large corporations) is incorporated in Delaware even though its headquarters and several of its major plants are in the state of Michigan.

Corporations that are organized under the laws of one state may operate in all or any other states. A corporation that does business in this way is referred to as a "foreign" corporation by the other state. One important fact that such foreign corporations must take into account is that they may have to qualify in order to begin doing business in any state other than their home state. Thus, corporations engaged in a foreign jurisdiction will be subject to that state's terms and conditions on foreign corporations before they will be permitted to engage in business in the state. This commonly entails a corporation's registering with the secretary of the state(s) where it must qualify (licensing). The tricky part is that there is no easily understood or universally accepted definition of that key phrase, *doing business*. The one certainty is that state laws do not define this phrase in the same way that the average businessperson would define it.

Corporations engaged in interstate commerce do not have to worry about this problem unless their business also involves substantial intrastate activities. They are protected by Article I, Sections 8 and 9 of the U.S. Constitution, which give Congress the responsibility for regulating interstate commerce and prohibit the states from interfering with such commerce. But in other instances, especially where a corporation engages in what is essentially intrastate commerce in two or more states, individual state laws apply. The question remains, what constitutes doing business within another state?

Ordinarily, maintaining a bank account in the foreign jurisdiction will not constitute doing business in the state. Neither will creating (as borrower or lender) or acquiring indebtedness, mortgages, or other security interests in real or personal property. Similarly, securing or collecting debts or enforcing any rights in property or effecting sales through independent contractors will not constitute doing business. An isolated transaction, which amounts to less than a substantial part of the business, generally won't require qualification. Even the holding of shareholders' or directors' meetings in the state won't constitute "doing business." Neither will the installation of equipment or the mere solicitation of stock subscriptions generally trigger licensing. On the other hand, maintaining an office or place of business within a state will be indicative (albeit not conclusive) that the foreign corporation is doing business there.

An insightful guideline is offered by an often-quoted 1942 decision in Alabama: "It is established by well considered general authorities that a foreign corporation is doing, transacting, carrying on or engaging in business within a state when it transacts some substantial part of its ordinary business therein."

If a corporation is doing "substantial" business in a state or states other than its home state, it must be in compliance with the statutes of the state(s) in question. Since most businesspeople do not have the time or the expertise to take on the task of checking the out-of-state corporate statutes, it follows that in cases where there is substantial doubt about whether qualification is necessary, the corporate officers or directors should consult qualified legal counsel.

Failure to qualify may result in a state's fining or otherwise penalizing a foreign corporation. In extreme cases, directors or officers may be found liable for any failure to comply with laws. For example, Oregon law subjects directors, officers, and agents to fines and/or imprisonment.

Perhaps more importantly, a corporation may not be recognized by the courts of the foreign state, and thus find it difficult to enforce its contracts, collect its debts, and otherwise act as a full-fledged corporate citizen of the state. Note that the validity of the contracts entered into by the corporation will not be impaired. The corporation may defend an action based on a contract, but it may not maintain an action until it has obtained a certificate of authority. This bar is substantive in nature and applies to a diversity action brought in federal court.

Before leaving the subject of operating outside one's domicile, it is worth noting that it is often less expensive to incorporate in a foreign jurisdiction than to qualify to do business there. Further, some states, like California, have pseudo-foreign corporation statutes that require corporations that are incorporated in another state but are principally located in California to comply with the essential features of California statutes. If there are any doubts about these issues, the problem should be discussed with counsel.

19

CORPORATE FINANCE: AN OVERVIEW

Insofar as corporate finance is concerned, there are basically two kinds of securities, debt securities and equity securities. A debt security represents that the corporation has borrowed funds from the secured party and is obligated to repay them. An equity security is an instrument representing an investment in the business in which the shareholder becomes an owner of the corporation. The totality of the enterprise's debt and equity securities is known as the capital structure. Those interested in security transfer issues should be certain to consult Article 8 of the Uniform Commercial Code (UCC), which has been adopted by all states except Louisiana and governs the original issue and transfer of not only stock, but also of all corporate securities. For a restriction on the right to transfer shares to be valid and enforceable, the owner's consent to the restriction must be obtained and the restriction must be reasonable. Transferees of shares of corporate stock will be bound by restrictions on their right to "alienate" such shares if they take the shares with notice of the restriction.

Debt Securities. An important consideration for growing

businesses is how to secure the cash needed both for operating and for capital expenses. Short-term loans are useful, for example, in financing receivables for short periods. If a corporation's credit standing is good, a bank may lend the funds on an unsecured basis. The bank may be willing to establish a line of credit in favor of the corporation by committing itself for a specified period to granting loans up to a fixed maximum amount. Such a line of credit may avoid delays in consummating loans when there is an immediate need for cash.

Especially with newer ventures, however, a bank may require that the loan be guaranteed by one or more principal shareholders. This can be done without jeopardizing either the corporation's status as an independent legal entity or the limited liability of the shareholders (other than making them personally responsible for the specific debts involved). Debts can also be secured by a lien against some of the corporation's assets. Such security may be required even when the borrower has a good credit history. An assignment of accounts receivable is a form of security routinely used.

Debt financing is valuable because of the concept of leverage. Leverage (or "trading on the equity") applies when the corporation is able to earn more on the borrowed capital than the total cost of that capital. These excess earnings increase the corporation's total rate of return on the invested capital. This is particularly true with long-term borrowing, which can finance additional plant and equipment. Of course, if a corporation over-expands, borrowing too much money and not earning enough to pay off the debt, the leverage works the other way, perhaps leading to bankruptcy.

Types of Debt Securities. *Debentures* are typically unsecured obligations involving only the personal obligation of the obligor with longer terms than other unsecured indebtedness.

Bonds are debt obligations generally understood to be backed by collateral, perhaps a mortgage against real estate or a lien on other fixed assets. Due to the presence of the security interest, the interest rate on bonds is usually lower than on debentures, and the bond maturity may be longer. Bonds are often bearer instruments, meaning that they are negotiable by delivery with the interest payments represented by coupons that are submitted for payment. Notes are generally payable to the order of a party and the interest payments are contractual obligations not represented by a coupon. Note that bonds may also be registered with an issuer and transferred only by endorsement. Article 8 of the Uniform Commercial Code makes registered bonds negotiable. A debenture or bond is usually issued under an indenture or trust agreement between the corporation and the trustee. The indenture contains restrictive covenants or negative pledges and confers powers on the trustee that are intended for the protection of the holders of the obligations.

Smaller corporations tend to make extensive use of term loans. Such loans may be arranged for varied periods, although banks often will not lend for more than five years on such a basis. With a term loan, the terms and conditions are set forth in an agreement which may also contain covenants restricting the borrower in the conduct of the business. Thus, there may be a requirement that working capital be maintained at a specified minimum level. Further, the agreement may contain negative covenants under which the borrower agrees not to create or permit to exist any mortgage, lien, or other encumbrance against its business assets, except those incurred in the ordinary course of business. Or the corporation might agree not to incur capital expenditures or to make loans or advances to others in excess of specified amounts.

Note that debt securities are generally subject to redemption and that the securities chosen for redemption may be chosen by lot or by some other means. Debt securities can be converted into equity securities such as common stock on some predetermined basis. When the convertible debentures are converted, they — and the related debt — disappear with the new securities (called the conversion securities) issued in their place. Convertible debentures are usually redeemable. Although the RMBCA does not give debenture holders the power to vote, it should be noted that some states permit holders of bonds to participate in the election of the directors either generally or upon particular contingencies such as a default in payment.

Equity Financing, or Stock. The restrictions that often accompany debt financing may lead to a decision to avoid a loan agreement and to obtain permanent financing instead through the sale of stock. Equity securities, which give the holders a share of the corporation, generally have no fixed maturity and contain no restrictions on the conduct of the business.

Types of Stock. There are two general types of conventional equity securities — common stock and preferred stock — although certain forms of hybrid securities exist as well combining features of debt securities and of shares. Whether hybrid securities are treated for tax purposes as debt or equity generally depends on whether there is a fixed maturity, a fixed return, and ranking with respect to general credit. Note that companies with only one class of stock are said to have only common stock as evidenced by a certificate. Recognition of the shareholder's status as such generally depends on record ownership.

The types and characteristics of stock and the implications of distributing shares in a corporation are described in the next key (20). In brief, common stock is generally characterized by the fact that its rate of return is not fixed. Dividends may be increased or decreased or even omitted depending on the company's performance. But common stockholders own a share of the business and are entitled to vote their shares in the election of directors and on other matters brought before the shareholders. Holders of common stock are entitled to the net assets of the corporation, after allowance for debt and senior securities, either during the life of the corporation (under certain circumstances) or, more commonly, during liquidation. Preferred stock generally pays dividends at a fixed rate and has preference over common stock in such payments and in any distribution of the corporation's assets.

20

ISSUANCE OF STOCK

All for-profit corporations issue stock that represents shares of ownership in the enterprise. The stock is given in exchange for money, property, or services. Thus, in setting up a corporation that will issue 1,000 shares of common stock, the incorporators may issue themselves each 400 shares in exchange for services performed; they may issue 150 shares to an investor who provides funds for them to purchase needed machinery and materials; and they may issue 50 shares to a real estate owner who deeds over to them a building in which they can set up their factory.

There are two major types of stock, common and preferred. Within these categories there are many types and classes of stock, some which can be used even by small, new corporations to accomplish various objectives, such as keeping control in the hands of the founders.

Common Stock. If a corporation has only one type of stock, it is common stock. The rate of return on common stock is not fixed; dividends are declared by the board of directors and generally depend on corporate performance. Under the RMBCA, there are two basic attributes of common stock. First, holders of common stock are entitled to vote for the election of directors and on other corporate matters. Second, holders of common stock as a group are entitled to all the net assets of the corporation (after making allowance for debt and senior securities) when distributions are made, either during the life of the corporation or during liquidation.

Under the RMBCA, these two characteristics may be divided between different classes of stock so that there may be no single class of stock that can clearly be said to be the only "common stock." Nevertheless, the RMBCA provides that at least one share of each class with either of these attributes must be outstanding. Various state laws enable corporations to create classes of common stock with distinct rights or privileges. Thus, Class A stock might be entitled to two votes per share, and Class B stock might be entitled to one vote per share. Or Class A stock might be entitled to elect more directors than Class B stock or be entitled to greater dividends.

Thus, common stock may be either voting or nonvoting, which is important for purposes of establishing corporate control within a particular group. It should be noted, however, that in some states the right to vote cannot be denied a class of stock and special rules apply where organic (fundamental) changes in the corporation are contemplated.

Preferred Stock. In general, preferred stock may be voting or nonvoting and is entitled to a preference in the distribution of dividends and/or in the assets of the business upon the liquidation of the corporation. Hence, the term "preferred" refers to the right to receive payment (either as a fixed dividend or as a liquidating distribution or both) before the common shareholders receive anything. In general, preferred shares contain both preferences.

Preferred shares may also be participating or nonparticipating. Both these types are entitled to a particular dividend before anything is paid out on the common shares, but only *participating* preferred shares are also entitled, after the common shareholders receive a stated amount, to share with them in subsequent distributions. Preferred dividends are generally cumulative; if a dividend is not paid during a year, that dividend will not be lost but will "cumulate" (i.e., will be regarded as a corporate debt, until it is paid). Thus, the preferred shareholders must receive all of their accumulated dividends, as well as their current dividend, before the common shareholders receive any dividends. Moreover, if there are unpaid cumulative dividends at the time of liquidation, they must be paid first before there is any distribution of assets to the remaining shareholders.

Preferred shares may be *redeemable* — that is, the corporation may buy them back — at a stated price. Further, they may be convertible, at the option of the shareholder, into common stock, at a stated ratio or price. Generally, the price of the common shares must appreciate significantly before it becomes profitable for preferred shareholders to convert their stock. Once the shares have been converted, they are "canceled," which means that they are returned to the status of authorized but unissued shares. Ordinarily, preferred shares are nonvoting, but this must be stated in the articles of incorporation, or else the preferred shareholders might be allowed to vote in proportion to the number of preferred shares outstanding.

Authorized Shares. A corporation is empowered to issue the number of shares authorized in the articles. This is known as the corporation's authorized stock or authorized capital. Generally, there is no upper limit on the number of shares that may be authorized. Thus, a company could authorize a million shares even though it intended to issue only 100. Authorized stock is not capital stock; the latter is based on the number of shares outstanding, those actually issued. Authorizing additional shares over what is needed immediately allows for contingencies and eliminates the necessity to amend the articles later if more capital is needed. On the other hand, authorizing an excessive number of shares may cause concern to investors, who may fear that authorized shares may be subsequently issued by the board without shareholder approval. In addition, some states base their stock or franchise taxes on the number of shares authorized.

Issued Shares. The process by which all or part of the corporation's authorized stock is sold is known as the issuance of shares. Such issuance requires action by the board accepting an offer to subscribe for shares of the corporation, then directing the secretary to issue appropriate share certificates upon receipt of the stated consideration. Prior to incorporation, subscription agreements may be made obligating the subscriber to purchase, and the new corporation to sell, the particular shares.

Par Value. Although the RMBCA omits the principle of par value in its treatment of authorized shares, many jurisdictions still reflect this concept, which is simply an arbitrary value assigned to a share. At one time, par value represented the actual selling price of the shares, but today it is of far more limited significance. In the context of par value stock, when the value of the consideration — whether cash or some other form of payment — received is less than the par value, the stock is said to be "watered" stock. Such stock is not deemed fully paid and nonassessable, and the shareholder may be liable for the difference between the par value and the amount paid. The classic watered-stock situation arises when a promoter transfers to the corporation overvalued property in exchange for par value stock in the corporation. Thus, par value represents a floor beneath which shares may not be issued. In the case of "no par" shares, the consideration is set without regard to a minimum imposed by par value.

Stated Capital. A concept that is closely related to par and no-par value is that of minimum capital and stated capital. The trend in state laws is not to require any particular amount of minimum capital—although there clearly must be some initial capital. The level of capital actually necessary is relevant for determining whether the business was so underfunded that the corporate veil can be pierced (see Key 12). Technically, what is known as stated capital must be at a level that it cannot be considered to be impaired; thus, it must afford at least some protection to creditors.

What is stated capital? Under Florida law, for example, it is the sum of the par value of the outstanding par shares plus the total consideration received for all the no-par shares (excepting the portion transferred to capital surplus), plus any amounts transferred to stated capital on the issuance of shares either as stock dividends or otherwise. In a no-par offering, Florida law provides that the entire consideration received constitutes the stated capital. The board may allocate to capital surplus any portion of this consideration for the issuance of shares without par value, subject to certain exceptions.

For example, assume that Jones buys all of the assets of the Darby Corporation, paying $50,000 in cash and giving a note for $150,000. Jones then decides to incorporate. (Normally he would have incorporated first.) He transfers all of the Darby assets and liabilities in a bill of sale to the new corporation, complies with any bulk transfer tax, and receives the stock. Presumably, the fair value of that stock would be $50,000. Assuming a par value of $1.00 per share, with Jones receiving 100 shares, the total par value would be $100. The difference between that amount and the $50,000 fair value, $49,900, would be allocated to surplus. Jones has stock worth $50,000, and the corporation has $50,000 of capital and $150,000 of liabilities. The corporation also has $200,000 in assets—the amount Jones paid for the Darby assets.

Having bought a company's assets, the buyer is entitled to a "fresh start," so that he can depreciate the purchased assets to the extent of their value. Had Jones purchased Darby's stock instead of its assets, there would be no such fresh start. (Among other problems that may be connected with the purchase of stock, the buyer may find that he has also acquired certain liabilities of the corporation, such as for back wages or taxes. This and other possible pitfalls can be covered in the contract of sale, but with the purchase of assets, one can generally see what one is getting.)

In a purchase of assets it is generally to the buyer's advantage to allocate as much as possible to the tangible, depreciable assets and as little to goodwill, etc., while the seller's advantage lies in the opposite direction, in order to minimize any gain—hence tax—on the sale. This is a matter to be negotiated as part of the sales agreement—but there is no guarantee that the IRS will accept the valuations specified in the agreement. The best practice is to obtain expert appraisals of the assets, so as to have an objective opinion of their value. In any event, both buyer's and seller's attorneys should review the contract of sale carefully, providing any contingency clauses that the parties agree on.

Consideration for Shares. Generally speaking, shares are issued for cash. However, other forms of consideration are possible. Many jurisdictions distinguish between eligible and ineligible consideration. Future labor, future services, and future payments (e.g., promissory notes) are ineligible unless stock is purchased by an officer, director, or employee of the corporation under a plan, agreement, or transaction, and the board reasonably expects such to benefit the corporation. In this case, the share certificates are retained by the corporation until the promissory notes are paid.

The RMBCA takes a more liberal view of eligible consideration. The RMBCA provides that the board may authorize shares to be issued for consideration consisting of any tangible or intangible property or benefit to the corporation, including cash, promissory notes, services performed, contracts for services to be performed, or other securities of the corporation. Since a problem may arise if the shares are issued and the services are not performed, if the future benefits are not received, or if the notes are not paid, the RMBCA provides that the corporation may escrow the shares until the services or benefits are performed or the notes paid.

Under the older MBCA, before the corporation issues the shares, the board must determine that the consideration received or to be received is adequate. The board's determination as to the adequacy of consideration is conclusive. Once the full consideration is received, the shares are paid-up and nonassessable. The RMBCA merely requires the board to find that the consideration received or to be received is adequate. The shareholder will generally not be personally liable for the acts or debts of the corporation except by virtue of his or her own acts or conduct.

Share Certificates. Under the RMBCA, shares may or may not be represented by certificates. If certificates are issued, each one must contain on its face the following information: the name of the issuer and that it is organized under the laws of the state involved; the name of the person to whom the shares are issued; and the number and class of shares and the designation of the series, if any, the certificate represents. (In complex corporate organizations classes of stock are divisible into series, which means that they may be convertible at different ratios and that they can pay dividends at different rates, offer distinct redemption rights, and provide varying rules for liquidation payments.) Alternatively, under the RMBCA, the certificate may state conspicuously that the corporation will furnish the shareholder this information in writing and without charge.

Stock certificates must be signed either manually or by facsimile by two officers designated in the bylaws or by the board and may bear the corporate seal or its facsimile. If the person who signed a share no longer holds office when the certificate is issued, the certificate is nevertheless valid.

Treasury Stock. Subject to state law, the corporation may decide to repurchase its shares. It may either cancel the shares, returning them to the category of authorized but unissued shares, or it may hold the repurchased shares as treasury stock. Thus, treasury shares are those shares that have been issued and were once outstanding but have been reacquired by the corporation and held in its treasury. Generally, there are statutory limitations on the ability of a corporation to reacquire its own shares. For example, a corporation generally may not acquire its own shares if it is insolvent or if the acquisition would render it insolvent. In this connection, it is useful to distinguish between insolvency in the "bankruptcy sense" and in the "equity sense." In the bankruptcy sense, a corporation is insolvent if its liabilities exceed its assets. In the equity sense, a corporation is insolvent if it is unable to meet its debts as they come due. Generally, a corporation may not reacquire its shares if it is insolvent — or would be rendered insolvent — in either sense.

21

S CORPORATIONS

One of the problems associated with regular (C) corporations is that they are considered taxable entities separate and apart from their owners. This is the origin of the term "double taxation" because corporate income is often taxed twice — first at the corporate rate and second at the individual rate, when dividends are distributed to shareholders. In an S corporation, on the other hand, items of income or loss pass through directly to shareholders, allowing them to avoid double taxation and to offset losses against income generated outside of the corporation. The character of individual items is maintained so that a corporate capital gain becomes an individual capital gain, tax-exempt income keeps its status at the shareholder level, and so on.

Since the enactment of the 1986 Tax Reform Act lowered the maximum individual rate below the maximum corporate rate, S corporation status has become more attractive for businesses generating taxable income. Generally, the higher a corporation's taxable income, the more likely S corporation status will be beneficial even if part of the earnings are retained in the business. On the flip side, if business losses are expected, the S election is also attractive, since the losses pass through to the shareholders, who are permitted to deduct their share of the loss in figuring adjusted gross income.

Although today's laws have made the partnership and the S corporation equal in most ways, some significant differences remain between the two forms. Thus, in the case of a tax loss, members of a firm or shareholders in a corporation can deduct such losses only to the extent of their basis (their investment) in the partnership or corporate stock. The difference is that the members of a partnership may each include their share of the partnership's liabilities, but shareholders in an S corporation may not count their share of the corporation's liabilities, in computing their basis. Thus, in such cases, shareholders get less benefit from a tax loss than do partners.

Another difference in the taxation of partnerships and S corporations lies in the fact that special allocations of a partnership's income may be made so long as the allocations have a substantial economic effect. An allocation has a substantial economic effect if it reflects the true economic arrangement of the partners and if it affects the dollar amount received by the partners to the same extent as the allocation. Since all shares in an S corporation must have an equal right to income, special allocations are not permissible.

Professional corporations should generally opt for the regular corporate form since all of the net income of the business is generally payable to the professional in the form of salary except for that portion the professional finds it more profitable to retain in the corporation. Moreover, an important reason for incorporating a professional's business is to obtain a business deduction for amounts paid for fringe benefits such as group life insurance. In an S corporation, such deductions are not ordinarily available for anyone who owns more than 2% of the shares in the corporation.

There are various technical distinctions between C and S corporations. As an example, loans from a qualified employee plan to plan participants are legal in a C corporation but are prohibited in an S corporation. Also, an S corporation may have no more than 35 shareholders, all of whom must be "natural persons," estates, or certain trusts such as the voting trust and the so-called Subchapter S trust. Corporations and partnerships may not be shareholders in an S corporation, nor may shareholders be nonresident aliens. Each individual who owns stock in an S corporation as a tenant in common, joint tenant, or tenant by the entirety is ordinarily considered a separate shareholder, but a husband and wife (and their estates) will be treated as a single shareholder.

Only domestic (U.S.) corporations may elect S corporation status. Further, certain specialized entities, such as insurers and banks that are entitled to special tax benefits not available to individuals, are ineligible to become S corporations. Moreover, a corporation may not elect S corporation status if it belongs to a group in which one or more corporations are connected through stock ownership with a common parent corporation.

An S corporation may have only one class of stock, so that dividend rights and liquidation preferences are equal for all shares. The stock may have differences in voting rights and still be considered a single class of stock if all other rights are identical. Nor will straight debt be regarded as a second class of stock. ("Straight debt" is a safe harbor device defined as any written, unconditional promise to pay a certain sum of money on demand or on a specified date so long as the interest rate and interest payment dates of the debt instrument are not contingent on the S corporation's profits, the borrower's discretion, or similar factors.) Further, the debt instrument cannot be converted directly or indirectly into stock, and the creditor must be eligible to own S corporation stock.

The actual election to become an S corporation is made by filing IRS Form 2555. All shareholders must consent to the election, either on the form or on separate declarations. (If any stock is held by a trust, the consent must be made and signed by the persons deemed to be the owners of the stock.) The election may be made on any date until the fifteenth day of the third month of the taxable year in which it is to be effective. A new corporation should file before the fifteenth day of the third month after the first date on which the corporation has shareholders, acquires assets, or begins business.

The taxable year of an S corporation must be either the

calendar year or another accounting period for which the corporation establishes a satisfactory business purpose. For instance, an S corporation may adopt a fiscal year if 25% or more of the corporation's gross receipts for the 12-month period is recognized in the last two months of the period; this requirement must be met for three consecutive 12-month periods.

Section 1244 permits ordinary loss treatment, subject to limitations, for losses on the sale or worthlessness of corporate stock. Since the amount of loss is the difference between the shareholder's basis in the stock and the amount received for the stock, shareholders of regular corporations who own Section 1244 stock should consider the implications of an S election on their basis in such stock. Any losses and deductions of an S corporation, including capital losses, pass through to the shareholders and reduce their basis in the S corporation stock. Thus, any loss on the sale of Section 1244 stock will be reduced by the amount of passed-through losses. It should be noted that losses and deductions of an S corporation are passed through and recognized by the shareholders at the close of the tax year of the S corporation in which they are incurred while a loss on Section 1244 stock is recognized only when the stock is sold or exchanged.

Every S corporation must file a return on Form 1120S each tax year, even though it may not be subject to tax. The corporation must report gross income and allowable deductions, as well as information concerning the shareholders, their holdings, and any distributions made on their pro rata shares of corporate items. If the return is based on a calendar year, it must be filed by March 15 following the close of the tax year. If an S corporation is permitted to use a fiscal year as its tax year, the return must be filed by the fifteenth day of the third month following the close of the fiscal year.

22

COMPENSATION PLANNING

One of the more important tax issues facing closely held corporations relates to compensation planning. Shareholders clearly have an objective in reducing corporate taxable income in order to eliminate the problem of double taxation — first at the corporate level and then at the shareholder level.

This can be accomplished in a number of ways. Earnings can be accumulated in the business itself, but this can lead to an accumulated earnings tax. The corporation may be thinly capitalized and thus make tax-deductible interest payments in lieu of nondeductible dividends, but there are debt-equity problems associated with this approach. Shareholders may lease assets such as real estate to the corporation, but this is fraught with difficulties. Active shareholders can increase their compensation, but as will be demonstrated, such compensation may be found to be unreasonable compensation.

The tax law permits reasonable allowances for compensation for personal services actually rendered. If compensation is unreasonable, it is treated as a nondeductible dividend. For this purpose, a person's total compensation is considered (i.e., not just salary but fringe benefits, pension and profit-sharing plans, and other compensation.) The burden of proof for deductibility is on the taxpayer.

For purposes of showing that compensation is unreasonably high, the IRS may argue that the return on capital to the shareholders is too low. Note that shareholders in the closely held corporation are somewhat less likely than shareholders in the publicly held corporation to challenge unreasonable compensation as a waste of corporate assets. However, the IRS challenges with some regularity what it considers to be excessive compensation. Three criteria are particularly relevant for determining whether compensation is unreasonable: the relationship of ownership to compensation; compensation paid for similar services in the same industry; and evidence that the compensation package was the product of arm's-length negotiation. For this purpose, written employment contracts can be useful if executed before the services are actually rendered. Generally, in addition to current compensation, such agreements cover deferred compensation, disability pay, death benefits, expense account issues, noncompetition clauses, eligibility for company benefit plans, and other matters. Given their legal and tax consequences, employment agreements should be reviewed carefully with counsel.

Other factors that can be relevant in determining if compensation was reasonable include the training and experience of the employee, whether the company had a reasonable dividend history, the job functions performed by the employee, the fact that the shareholder left a high-paying job to take his current one, and the size of the business. Further, it is better to pay compensation as salary rather than as a bonus. Sometimes shareholder-employees are paid according to contingent-compensation arrangements, such as those that are based on net profits at the end of the year. So long as the employee's contract was reasonable at the time the contract for services was made, it should be able to survive IRS scrutiny.

Factors tending to support characterizing a payment as a dividend rather than as a salary include poor dividend histories, discrepancies between compensation to insiders and compensation to outsiders for the same services rendered, and the relation between compensation and ownership. Thus, if four 25% shareholders with different jobs receive the same salaries, this could pose a problem. Similarly, bonus payments are very troublesome, especially if they are determined late in the year for apparent tax-planning purposes.

To solve this problem of unreasonable compensation, the corporation may enter into so-called hedge agreements with employees, indicating that any portion of the compensation that is subsequently disallowed as a deduction for the corporation will be repaid to the corporation on a tax-free basis under the tax-benefit rule, with a deduction allowed the employee. The problem is that the mere existence of such agreements may weaken the argument that the compensation was reasonable (if management took account of the risk, there must be cause for such concern). However, the IRS may validate such agreements so long as they are enforceable under state law.

As a final consideration, it should be noted that unreasonably low salaries paid to reduce social security taxes or for some other reason may pose a problem. An allocation of additional compensation is particularly likely for sole or controlling shareholders. A related issue is that of below-market loans made to employees and independent contractors to avoid the application of rules relating to the payment of employment taxes and rules on the deductibility of interest. Those interested in this topic will want to review the complex provisions wrought by the 1986 Tax Reform Act in the area of interest-free and below-market-rate-of-interest loans.

23

FRINGE BENEFITS

One of the major benefits of the corporate form of business organization is that fringe benefits such as insurance can be provided to employees (and officers) without the recipients having to pay taxes on the value of the benefits. Key 24, INSURANCE ARRANGEMENTS, deals with major ways of providing protection for employees and their families.

In this key we will consider various other fringe benefits that can also be important. Employees may exclude from gross taxable income the value of any meals and lodging furnished to them by or on behalf of the employer if furnished on the business premises or for the convenience of the employer. (Ministers of the gospel and employees of educational institutions can exclude the value of housing provided to them.)

Stock options can be an important way to compensate key people. Such options enable employees to become owners of the business at favorable prices. The option is granted to buy stock at a specified price level, and can be exercised at a later point in time. The idea is that the stock of a growing company will rise over a period of time, so that by the time the holder is ready to exercise his option, the stock's market price will be significantly higher than the option price. As a practical matter, stock options only have limited use for closely held corporations, since the stock of small corporations generally does not have a readily ascertainable fair market value. In addition, the owners do not generally wish to dilute their ownership by issuing additional stock.

Another formerly prominent fringe relates to interest-free and below-market-rate loans made by the corporation to the employee. The current law still offers favorable treatment to such arrangements, but only in the case of a demand loan, a loan that is payable in full at any time on the demand of the lender. The loan is measured against an objective standard known as the applicable federal rate, which is published monthly. Overall, the rules and standards for demand and term loans are complex, and should be reviewed by a competent attorney or accountant.

Another set of employee fringe benefits includes several classes of excludable benefits provided by employers. The first of these is *for-no-additional-cost services*. To be nontaxable, such services must be offered to customers in the ordinary course of the business in which the employee works, and the employer must not incur substantial additional costs by providing the service to the employee (an example is providing free air travel where the seat would otherwise be empty). The next fringe is qualified *employee discounts,* such as for apparel in department stores. When an employer sells goods or services to the employee at a price below its going value, the law permits the employee to exclude the discount from income subject to certain limitations (e.g., the goods or services must be from the same line of business in which the employee works).

The next benefit, called the *working-condition fringe,* holds that an employee is not required to include in income the cost of goods or services provided if the employee could have deducted the cost of these items had he actually paid for them. Such fringes may not be used to benefit members of the employee's family. Examples of working-condition fringes include subscriptions to business publications, bodyguard services, free or low-cost parking, and use of a company automobile or airplane by the employee for business purposes. The value of the use of consumer goods for product testing and evaluation purposes by an employee outside the workplace is also excludable as a working-condition fringe since consumer testing and evaluation of a product is an ordinary and necessary business expense of the employer. In this connection, the value of qualified automobile demonstration use is also excludable from income as a working condition fringe. This term refers to any use of a demonstration automobile by a full-time automobile salesman in the sales area in which the dealer's sales office is located. The use must be provided primarily to facilitate the employee's sales performance, and there must be substantial restrictions placed on the personal use of the car.

The *de minimis* fringes include benefits so small in value that accounting for them would be unreasonable or administratively impractical (e.g., the cost of typing a personal letter by a company secretary). To determine whether the de minimis fringe exclusion applies, one takes into consideration the frequency with which these and similar benefits are provided by the employer to the employees, since this issue may bear on whether the fair market value of the benefits is so small as to make accounting for them impractical.

Another fringe in this area, especially for larger corporations, is subsidized *eating facilities*. Briefly, the excess of the value of meals consumed over the fee charged is nontaxable if the eating facility is located on or near the employer's premises, if the revenues derived normally equal or exceed the direct operating costs of the facility, and the nondiscrimination rules are satisfied. Neither is the employee required to include in gross income any amount relating to the use of an on-premises *athletic facilities* provided by the employer. The exclusion applies to a gym or other facility operated by the employer, substantially all of the use of which is by the employees, their spouses, *and* their dependents. Athletic facilities also include tennis courts, golf courses, and swimming pools. Other fringe benefits, such as for reduced tuition to an employee of an educational institution or for scholarships for employees' children, are also available under specified circumstances.

One of the most important powers of a corporation is the power to establish pension and other incentive and compensation plans. This power has implications not only for base compensation and fringe benefits but for more specialized topics like so-called cafeteria plans and golden parachute arrangements. The area of deferred compensation arrangements—both qualified and nonqualified—is highly complex because it requires an understanding of both the Employee Retirement Income Security Act (ERISA) and the Internal Revenue Code ("IRC"). For example, both ERISA and the IRC impose substantial reporting and disclosure obligations on covered plans. What follows is merely an overview of the issues.

It is important to distinguish between qualified and nonqualified plans. In a qualified plan, employer contributions are deductible from taxable income. In addition, the earnings of a qualified plan are exempt from income taxation, and the employer contributions are not taxable to the employees until they are received in the form of benefits, when they may qualify for favorable tax treatment.

For a plan to be treated as "qualified" under the IRC, it must be a plan of deferred compensation (i.e., the intent must be to defer receipt of compensation beyond the year in which it is earned). Other requirements include such items as the following: there must be a legally binding arrangement in writing and communicated to the employees; the plan must be for the exclusive benefit of a broad class of employees or their beneficiaries; the plan must not discriminate in favor of officers, stockholders, or highly compensated employees: the plan must satisfy certain minimum requirements related to participation and vesting; there must be limitations on maximum benefits; the plan must be permanent (i.e., it cannot be a temporary arrangement); there can be no diversion of fund assets or income; any life insurance benefits provided must be incidental; minimum funding standards must be observed; contributions must be made by the employer or employee or both; there must be applicable plan termination and merger and consolidation requirements; and the plan must satisfy Social Security integration rules.

Basically, there are three types of qualified plans—pension, profit-sharing, and stock bonus plans. A *pension plan* is a deferred compensation arrangement providing for systematic payment of definitely determinable retirement benefits to employees who satisfy the plan requirements, generally for life, following retirement. There are two broad categories of pension plans. One, the defined contribution plan, requires the amount contributed by the employer to be based on a flat dollar amount, a formula, a specified percentage of compensation, etc. Second, the defined benefit plan, defines the benefits employees will receive, with the employer required to make annual contributions based on actuarial contributions deemed sufficient to cover the retirement benefits. Separate accounts are not maintained for each participant.

A *profit-sharing plan* is a deferred compensation arrangement established and maintained by an employer to provide for employee participation in company profits. The employer is not required to contribute a definite, predetermined amount to the plan, although substantial and regular contributions must be made to satisfy the permanency requirement.

The *stock bonus plan* is a deferred compensation plan established and maintained to provide contributions of the employer's stock to the plan. Note that both profit-sharing plans and stock bonus plans are forms of defined contribution pension plans.

An *employee stock ownership plan* (ESOP) is a stock bonus trust, qualifying as tax exempt, established to invest primarily in qualifying employer securities. The corporation receives a tax deduction equal to the fair market value of the stock contributed.

A qualified profit-sharing or stock bonus plan may include a qualified cash or deferred arrangement ("CODA"). Under a CODA or Section 401(k) plan, an employee may elect to have the employer make payments either as contributions to the plan on behalf of the employee or directly to the employee as cash. Plan contributions are taxed only when ultimately distributed from the plan.

Contributions may be either elective or nonelective. Elective contributions are amounts that the employee may elect to receive as an immediate cash payment or have the employer contribute on his or her behalf. Nonelective contributions are amounts that the employer puts directly in the plan on the employee's behalf and that the employee cannot receive as a direct payment (e.g., a matching payment by the employer of 30 cents for every dollar the employee elects to defer). Most employers provide a matching contribution as an incentive to employee participation. Interestingly, although elective deferrals are not includible in the employee's gross income, such contributions are considered as wages for Social Security purposes. Moreover, some state and local taxing authorities may not grant tax-favored status to such payments.

The subject of benefit plans is wide-ranging and complex, worthy of a separate book. In this key we have given an overview, suggesting areas worth further investigation by business owners and their advisers.

24

INSURANCE ARRANGEMENTS

Insurance is important to any closely held corporation for several reasons. One advantage is that a corporation can provide accident and health insurance for its employees on a tax-favored basis, because the premium payments are deductible by the corporate payer but are not included in the employee's income. Further, a medical reimbursement plan can permit employees to exclude from income amounts received under a plan as reimbursement for medical expenses incurred for their own medical care as well as care for their spouses and dependents. This should be compared to individual taxpayers, who can deduct medical insurance premiums only to the extent that such payments, along with other medical expenses, exceed 7.5% of adjusted gross income.

Life insurance can also play an important role in a closely held corporation, quite apart from buy-sell agreements or more complex arrangements such as funding a Section 303 redemption. For example, life insurance benefits may be provided in a qualified retirement plan if incidental to the primary purpose of the plan. This key is intended to explore some other applications of life insurance for closely held corporations — split-dollar insurance, executive bonus plans, corporate-owned insurance, and group life insurance.

In split-dollar insurance, the insured employee and the employer agree to share in the purchase of a permanent, not a term life insurance contract on the life of the employee.

The contractual arrangements vary, but generally the employer pays the portion of the premium equal to the annual increase in the cash surrender value of the policy and the employee pays the balance. Thus the employee's required contributions will be more in the early years of the policy, less as the policy value builds. On the employee's death, the employer receives the portion of the proceeds equal to the greater of the cash surrender value of the policy just prior to death or the total amount of premiums paid by the employer. The balance of the proceeds goes to the employee's named beneficiary. Other arrangements are possible, too.

Split-dollar insurance enables a large amount of low-cost life insurance to be provided when the employee can use it most. The corporation is thus able to give an employee the equivalent of a raise in salary without much extra cost, thus increasing its ability to attract and retain better employees. No IRS approval is required, and the plan can be used to supplement a group-term plan, a profit-sharing plan, or a pension plan.

Another use of life insurance entails the "executive bonus" plan. The employer takes responsibility for providing premium payments on policies on the lives of the employees, who own the policies, designate the beneficiary, and pay the premiums. The corporation pays a bonus to the employees to cover the cost of the premium; income tax must be paid on that bonus. No IRS approval is needed, so the plan is totally flexible — the employer can determine who will participate. There are no installation costs and no annual operating costs. The employer may not be a beneficiary directly or indirectly under the policy, and the premium must represent additional compensation for services rendered by the employee.

Another use of life insurance involves policies owned by, payable to, or for the benefit of the corporation. For example, such insurance can be used as a part of a key-man arrangement to provide funds for a deferred compensation or a stock redemption plan (e.g., to make provision for the key man's retirement or death.) A key man is any person who exerts a high degree of influence on the business. As an example, if a business has made a heavy commitment to expansion, the death of this key man before the expansion is complete could lead to financial ruin (e.g., the creditors may stop extending credit). Although the premium payments in such a plan are nondeductible, the proceeds received by the corporation upon the death of the shareholder are tax free, and even the "inside buildup" of the policy is tax free.

Another use of life insurance is the Section 79 or group term life insurance benefit. For many closely held corporations, this can represent an ideal fringe benefit. Simply put, to qualify as group insurance, under the law, the plan must establish a death benefit that is excludable from gross income (i.e., qualify as a life insurance contract), the life insurance must be provided to a group of employees, a master policy must be carried directly or indirectly by the corporate employer, and the insurance must be carried on a basis that prevents individual selection. This last might involve a formula taking into account such factors as age, years of service, compensation, or position. The tax result is that the employee will receive the first $50,000 of the cost of the coverage tax free with the excess taxable, computed pursuant to a special IRS table. An employee's contributions toward the costs of group term coverage will be credited to coverage in excess of the $50,000.

In sum, the employee receives a substantial economic benefit tax free, and the premium payments made should be deductible by the corporate payer. The law says that the plan may not discriminate in favor of key employees as to eligibility in the plan or as to plan benefits. Thus, where group plans of fewer than ten employees are involved, care must be exercised to make sure that the key employees will not have to report the full premium payment in income.

25

DIVIDENDS:
AN OVERVIEW

A dividend is any distribution of cash or property paid to shareholders on account of share ownership. Generally, dividends represent the portion of the corporation's profits that does not have to be retained in the treasury to finance expansion or for some other business purpose. It is up to the board of directors to decide when to declare dividends and in what form. Tax considerations are an important factor in such decisions, though less so in S corporations.

Distributions may be made in the company's own stock rather than in cash or property. A stock dividend (or share dividend) simply distributes additional shares among the shareholders. Since no cash or property is distributed, it does not reduce the true worth of the corporation or increase the true worth of the shareholder. It simply increases the number of shares outstanding without reducing assets. A stock dividend does affect stated capital (also called stated value), however. A stock dividend should be distinguished from a stock split, which divides the number of shares into a greater number and reduces proportionately the par value of the shares without affecting stated capital. Thus, no transfer from surplus to stated capital is required. (Note: as the RMBCA has eliminated the concept of par value, no distinction is made there between share dividends and stock splits.)

Once a dividend has been legally declared, the shareholder becomes a creditor of the corporation in the amount of the dividend. To determine which shareholders are entitled to a dividend, the board may set a "record date" unless the bylaws provide a method for fixing the date. All shareholders on record as of that date are entitled to payment. The "payment date" is the day payment is made, and the "date of declaration" refers to the day the board passes the appropriate resolution. Some state laws regulate the fixing of the record date. If the directors do not fix a record date at all, the dividend will belong to the owners of record as of the date of declaration, regardless of who owns the stock when the dividend is paid.

In most cases shareholders have no absolute right to the payment of dividends. The board alone is empowered to determine, in its best judgment, if and when dividends should be declared and in what amounts. That is, courts will not second guess the business judgment of directors if exercised in good faith or if based on the best available information. However, a shareholder may attempt to show that the board's refusal to declare a dividend was in bad faith or so unreasonable as to constitute an abuse of discretion. This can arise especially in closely held corporations, where majority interests may attempt to oppress the minority shareholders by refusing to declare dividends notwithstanding the existence of large surpluses. Under North Carolina law, the directors of a closely held corporation are required to justify their refusal to pay less than one-third of the net annual profits in dividends where holders of 20% or more of the shares object to the board's dividend policy. Relatedly, although preferred shareholders have no guaranteed right to dividends, the articles may give them this right if corporate earnings are sufficient for payment.

There are also restrictions as to what funds should be available for distribution. Generally, cash or property dividends are payable only out of surplus (i.e., an excess of net assets over stated capital). In some states, dividends cannot be paid out of stated capital. The reason for this is that the corporation's stated capital signifies amounts contributed by the shareholders to allow the corporation to operate. Creditors are permitted to rely on such amounts for payment of debts incurred by the business. Thus, directors are liable to the corporation for their declaration of unauthorized dividends.

If the capital account is impaired, whether through operating losses or some other cause, the corporation cannot declare a dividend even though it has current net profits. On the other hand, some states do allow payment of dividends out of current net profits, notwithstanding impairment of the capital account. Further, in California, a corporation may pay cash or property dividends so long as its total assets after the payment are at least equal to 1.25 times its liabilities and its current assets are at least equal to its current liabilities. Of course, no dividend may be paid contrary to any restrictions in the articles.

The MBCA provides that cash or property dividends may be declared so long as total assets are at least equal to total liabilities. For this purpose, the value of corporate assets may be based upon any fair value that is reasonable under the circumstances. There are also technical requirements related to payment of dividends out of various kinds of surplus (e.g., earned surplus, paid-in surplus). In any event, dividends are generally prohibited where the corporation is in fact insolvent or where payment of the dividend would render the corporation insolvent. Note that generally a repurchase or redemption will have the same effect as a dividend, so similar limitations apply. All of these actions represent a distribution of money to shareholders without any direct benefit to the corporation.

26

DIVIDENDS IN CASH OR PROPERTY

Corporate distributions of cash and property to shareholders are treated as ordinary income to the extent the corporation has accumulated earnings and profits. In finding the source of the distribution, a dividend is deemed initially to have been made from current earnings and profits.

The actual tax treatment depends not only on earnings and profits but also on the recipient shareholder's basis in the shares as follows:

1. The distribution is an ordinary dividend only to the extent of current earnings and profits.

2. If there are no current (i.e., this year's) earnings and profits, but there are accumulated earnings and profits from prior years, the distribution is taxable as an ordinary dividend to the extent of accumulated earnings and profits.

3. If there are neither current nor accumulated earnings and profits, the distribution is a nontaxable return of capital, with the recipient shareholders reducing their basis in the assets to the extent of the distribution.

4. If there are neither current nor accumulated earnings and profits, and the shareholder's basis in the shares is reduced to zero, the excess is taxed as a gain on the sale of the shares (ordinarily, at capital-gains rates.)

In sum, one must maintain two accounts for earnings and profits — one for the current year and one for all previous years. If either account shows a positive balance, the distribution is taxable as a dividend. If a distribution exceeds earnings and profits, however, such excess is not taxable as a dividend but is, as explained above, a reduction in basis. Once the basis is reduced to zero, the distribution is generally taxable as a capital gain. Calculating earnings and profits is a complex exercise, but the final amount roughly corresponds to the earned-surplus account, representing the retained profits from operations as well as various nonoperating items such as the sale of assets.

So much for cash dividends. Insofar as any property dividends — or dividends in kind — are concerned, a distribution of property to a noncorporate shareholder is measured by the fair market value of the property on the date of the distribution. The shareholder's basis in the property received is also the fair market value on the date of distribution. As is the case with cash dividends, the portion of the distribution covered by existing earnings and profits is treated as a dividend, with the excess considered a return of capital. If the fair market value of the property distributed exceeds the corporation's earnings and profits and the shareholder's basis in the stock, a capital gain results. The amount distributed is reduced by any liabilities to which the distributed property is subject immediately before and immediately after the distribution and by any liabilities of the corporation assumed by the shareholder in connection with the distribution.

Note that distributions of appreciated property may cause gain to the distributing corporation — as if the corporation had sold the property to its shareholders at a fair market value *higher than* the corporation's basis in the property. However, no loss is recognized to the distributing corporation on distributions of property with a tax basis in excess of the property's fair market value. If the distributed property is subject to a liability in excess of basis, or if the shareholder assumed such a liability, the fair market value of the property for purposes of determining gain (or loss) on the distribution

101

is considered as being not less than the amount of the liability.

Overall, in the event of a property distribution, the earnings and profits account is reduced by the amount of cash distributed or by the greater of either the fair market value or the adjusted basis of property distributed, less the amount of any liability on the property. Earnings and profits are increased by gain recognized on appreciated property distributed as a property dividend. Note that such distributions cannot trigger a deficit in earnings and profits; such a deficit can only result through the generation of business losses.

Another type of dividend is the so-called disguised or constructive dividend. Such dividends are not declared per se but result from a corporate action such as the payment of excessive salaries or distributions for the personal benefit of shareholders. Such payments are tantamount to dividends and are so treated by the IRS. Constructive dividends reduce the earnings and profits of the corporation but are not deductible for tax purposes. They have the same tax attributes as actual distributions. One must be careful in interpreting whether a payment qualifies as a disguised dividend. For example, if a corporation pays the premiums on key-man life insurance policies owned by shareholder-employees, an economic benefit has been conferred on these employees amounting to a constructive dividend. A different result would be reached where the corporation is deemed to own the policies, however. The central point, therefore, is whether or not a measurable economic benefit has been conferred on the shareholder.

Federal law requires payors of dividends or interest aggregating $10 or more in a calendar year to file an information return with the IRS. Withholding may also be required, as in cases where the payee has not submitted to the payer a correct tax identification number.

27

STOCK DIVIDENDS AND RIGHTS

There are many instances in which a corporation may have surplus profits but little or no cash available to pay dividends because the profits have been invested in additional inventory or fixed assets. The shareholders nevertheless may desire a distribution that will not affect the financial condition of the corporation, and for this purpose the directors may pay a dividend in its own stock.

Assume, for example, that a corporation with $10,000 of capital stock and $5000 of earned surplus can legally declare a dividend of 50%. Thus, it could increase its authorized capital stock to $15,000 and transfer $5000 from the earned surplus to the capital stock account. Stock will be issued to the shareholders at the rate of one share for every two shares held. Theoretically, the status of the shareholders and their individual interests in the corporation has not changed. Thus, a shareholder who owned 10% of the business prior to the dividend continues to own 10% of the business. The assets have not been increased or decreased in this balance-sheet transaction. Only the liabilities have changed, in that an item of surplus has been transformed into a liability (i.e., before the declaration of the dividend, a holder of $1000 in stock had

100 shares, theoretically worth $15 per share. Following the declaration of the stock dividend, the same shareholder holds 150 shares, theoretically worth $10 per share).

An understanding of the tax treatment of stock dividends and stock rights is pivotal for understanding the tax treatment of related matters such as stock redemptions (see Key 33). In general, stock dividends are not taxable if they are pro rata distributions of stock on common stock. There are five exceptions to this general rule, however:

1. Distributions payable either in stock or in property. If any stockholder is given the choice of accepting cash or property other than stock, all stockholders will be taxed on the stock dividend; however, this exception does not apply to certain dividend-reinvestment plans or to cash distributed in lieu of fractional shares. (In such cases the cash is generally not included in the stockholder's gross income.)

2. Distributions resulting in the receipt of property by some shareholders and an increase in the proportionate interest of other shareholders in the assets or earnings and profits of the distributing corporation. Distributions of stock and cash or property are considered disproportionate only if a stock dividend on the common stock is balanced by a cash or property distribution on preferred stock or debentures that are convertible into common stock — that is, if the distribution increases the proportionate interests of at least some class of the common shares.

3. Distributions that result in the receipt of preferred stock by some common stock shareholders and the receipt of common stock by other shareholders.

4. Distributions on preferred stock — whether actual or constructive, and whether or not the distribution has a disproportionate effect — other than an increase in the conversion ratio of convertible preferred stock made solely to take account of a stock dividend or stock split with respect to stock into which the preferred is convertible.

5. Distributions of convertible preferred stock, unless it can be proven that the distribution will not result in a disproportionate distribution. The IRS generally considers

such a disproportionate distribution to result when the conversion right must be exercised shortly after the date of the stock distribution and when the dividend rates, the redemption provisions, the marketability of the convertible stock, and the conversion price indicate that some shareholders will exercise their rights while others will not.

The rules governing the tax treatment of rights to purchase stock are basically the same as the rules for stock dividends. If the stock rights are taxable, the recipient has income to the extent of the fair market value of the rights. This fair market value then becomes the recipient's basis in the rights. If the rights are exercised and the recipient buys stock, the holding period for this stock is based on the date the rights — whether taxable or nontaxable — are exercised. The basis of the new stock is the basis of the rights plus the amount of any other consideration given up.

If the stock rights are not taxable at issuance and their value is less than 15% of the value of the existing stock, the basis of the rights is zero unless the shareholder elects to have some of the basis in the old stock allocated to the rights. If the fair market value of the rights is 15% or more of the value of the existing stock and the rights are exercised or sold, the shareholder must allocate the basis in the old stock between the stock itself and the rights in proportion to their relative market values on the distribution date. The purpose of this 15% demarcation is to avoid the necessity for having minimal basis adjustments on a distribution of rights of relatively small value.

A closely related subject is that of bond rights and warrants. Generally, when a shareholder receives rights to subscribe to bonds that are convertible into shares of stock, the rights will be nontaxable if a dividend paid on the stock into which the bonds are convertible would be a nontaxable stock dividend and the value of the rights is attributable to the conversion privilege. The basis is determined in the same manner as if it were new stock. Should the bonds be converted into stock, the basis of the new stock is the basis of the bonds plus any consideration paid at the time of the conversion. If the bonds are not convertible into stock, such rights are treated as property dividends. The basis of the shares remains unchanged, and the basis of the bonds is determined in the same manner as that of new stock.

It has been noted previously that a distribution is not an ordinary dividend if it is not paid out of the corporation's earnings and profits. In such cases it is treated as a return of the shareholder's investment. Such a return of capital is not taxed until the shareholder's basis in the stock has been fully recovered. To the extent a return of capital exceeds one's basis in the stock, it is included in the tax return as a capital gain.

Stockholders receive a liquidating dividend when the corporation redeems their stock in a partial or complete liquidation. Such stock may be redeemed for cash or for the corporation's assets. For a partial liquidation of stock, the tax treatment depends on whether or not a redemption of stock held by a noncorporate stockholder is essentially equivalent to a dividend. If it is, the distribution is treated as a dividend taxable to the shareholder, but any gain on any appreciated property included in the distribution is taxed to the corporation. For a complete liquidation, the amount received is treated as the proceeds from the sale of the redeemed stock by the shareholder. In computing the amount received, any property received is taken into consideration based on its fair market value. The amount of gain or loss is the difference between the basis of the redeemed stock and the amount received in liquidation. As the stock is a capital asset, the shareholder will have capital gain or loss unless an exception applies (e.g., the collapsible corporation rules). Whether the gain or loss is short- or long-term will depend on when the stock was acquired and for how long a period it was held.

28

TAXATION OF THE ENTREPRENEUR

This key will outline the tax treatment of the small business (S) corporation and the regular (C) corporation. The tax law allows S corporations to elect special tax treatment, so that tax at the corporate level is avoided. Instead, the income and expenses of the corporation are divided among the shareholders, who then report them on their own tax returns. Regular (C) corporations have their advantages too. For example, income splitting between the corporation and the individual can be accomplished through this form to shelter business income from the progressive rates applicable to individuals. As will be discussed later, however, although the regular corporation still offers certain tax-free benefits, such as group life insurance, not available to other forms, the advantages to a small business of operating as a regular corporation may be more apparent than real, in view of recent changes in the Internal Revenue Code.

The tax law imposes a tax on the taxable income of every corporation without defining the term. The Internal Revenue Code's definitional section states that the term *corporation* includes associations, joint stock companies, and insurance companies. The fact that a corporation is treated as such under state law is not necessarily determinative since the IRS classification is based on federal and not on state law. Under federal tax law, a corporation is an entity with associates, an objective of carrying on a business for profit and dividing the gains therefrom, continuity of life, centralized management, limited liability, and free transferability of interests. Sole proprietorships, business partnerships, and most trusts are not classified as corporations because they do not meet these criteria.

The S corporation law enables the owners of closely held corporations to avoid the double taxation of business income — once at the corporate level and again at the shareholder level — without loss of the corporate advantage of limited liability. S corporations are like partnerships in that most of the tax attributes pass through to the individual shareholders and are reported by them on their respective tax returns. If the business should experience losses, S corporation status allows the shareholders to use them to offset or shelter their other income. At-risk rules limit the amount of losses deductible by shareholders to the shareholder's basis in the stock, including such items as loans the shareholder makes to the corporation, and the net fair market value of personal assets that secure nonrecourse borrowing.

The passive activity loss rules limiting the deductibility of business losses also apply to S corporation shareholders who do not materially participate in the corporation's trade or business (and if no exceptions to the passive loss rules apply). Thus, such taxpayers can only offset losses of the business against other passive income (e.g., from the rental of property). Shareholders who materially participate in the S corporation's business can use their passive losses (and credits) to offset nonpassive income.

An S corporation must file a return on Form 1120S each year even though it may not be subject to tax. It reports gross income and allowable deductions, as well as information regarding the shareholders, their holdings, distributions, and pro rata shares of corporate items. The S corporation must furnish each shareholder with a copy of its return on or before the day the return is filed.

All S corporations generally must adopt the calendar year for federal tax purposes unless a bona fide business purpose can be shown to the satisfaction of the IRS that a fiscal year is justified. This change was intended to conform corporate tax years with those of the owners of the business.

The Tax Reform Act of 1986 made three important changes in the taxation of regular corporations which affect the selection of corporate form. First, the law generally made the top corporate rates higher than the top rates facing individuals. Corporate rates are 15% up to $50,000, 25% over $50,000 but not over $75,000, and 34% over $75,000. For corporations with taxable income of over $100,000, the benefit of the lower rates that apply to the first $75,000 is phased out by imposing a surcharge of 5% on taxable income over $100,000 and up to $335,000. Overall, individuals face a top tax rate of 28%. Under the Revenue Act of 1987, the taxable income of a qualified personal-service C corporation is taxed at a flat rate of 34%. In this connection, a personal service corporation is one in which substantially all of the activities involve the performance of services in the fields of health, law, engineering, architecture, accounting, actuarial science, performing arts, or consulting, and substantially all of the stock of which is held by employees or retired employees or their estates.

In any event, a corporation expected to have only taxable income of $75,000 or less might be better off staying with the regular corporate tax form to keep those favorable rates. However, regular corporations, like individuals, are now subject to a tough alternative minimum tax equal to the excess of the tentative minimum tax for the tax year over the regular tax. The tentative minimum tax for this purpose is 20% of the alternative minimum tax base reduced by the alternative minimum tax foreign tax credit.

The reader might be tempted to create as many corporations as possible, spreading out income in order to take advantage of the lower tax rates. However, a controlled group of corporations is allowed just one amount in each of the corporate rate brackets beneath the top bracket, which is divided equally among them or shared as they elect, along with a single maximum accumulated earnings tax credit. For this purpose, a controlled group is defined as either a parent-subsidiary group or a brother-sister group. Your tax adviser can help in defining these terms and other complex tax strategies beyond the scope of this book.

The second major change in corporate taxation brought about by the Tax Reform Act of 1986 provides for both a corporate-level as well as an individual-level tax on the liquidation of a corporation. Subject to certain exceptions, the law provides that gain or loss will be recognized to a liquidating corporation on the distribution of property to its shareholders in complete liquidation as if the property were sold at its fair market value. Gain or loss will also have tax consequences for shareholders when they receive the liquidating distributions. The imposition of a tax on the liquidating corporation, along with the increase in the capital gains tax rates, more than doubled the maximum federal tax rate on corporate liquidations compared to that existing prior to the 1986 Act. (See Key 40.)

A third major change wrought by the 1986 Act relates to net operating loss carryforwards. Before explaining these changes, some background information would be in order. First, every regular corporation must file an annual income tax return whether or not it has taxable income, and it must make estimated tax payments if its tax can reasonably be expected to be $40 or more. Corporations that receive articles of incorporation but never perfect their organization, transact business, or receive income may apply to the IRS to be relieved of filing.

A corporation not in existence an entire year is required to file a return for the part of the year it was in existence. This return must be filed on or before the 15th day of the third month following the close of the corporation's tax year. Corporations may receive an automatic extension of six months for filing the return by filing the prescribed form by the due date of the return. Corporations that are members of an affiliated group (those that are controlled through at least 80% ownership by the common parent and/or other members of the group, with the common parent directly controlling at least one subsidiary member) may elect to have their common parent file a single *consolidated return* for all of the members in lieu of separate tax returns by each. Note that every subsidiary must adopt the parent's accounting period the first year its income is included in the consolidated return. Generally, once a consolidated return is filed, the group must continue to file on a consolidated basis. A number of tax-saving benefits follow from filing a consolidated return. For instance, the operating losses of one group member may be offset against the operating profits of another, and intercompany profits and losses are not generally taken into income until ultimately realized in transactions with outsiders, and there is no tax on intercompany dividends. There are disadvantages to filing a consolidated return as well. For example, losses on intercompany transactions must be deferred, and consolidated income for tax purposes may differ from income for financial statement (book) purposes.

A new corporation can generally choose the fiscal year that most benefits its shareholders. Assume a corporation begins business on January 1 and elects a June 30 fiscal year. The resulting six-month deferral may reduce taxes significantly during the first year. However, personal service corporations are required to adopt a calendar year for tax purposes. (In such corporations the principal activity is the performance of personal services, substantially performed by owner–employees.) So, too, are most S corporations.

Gross income of a corporation, for federal tax purposes, consists not only of gross receipts from the sale of goods or services but also of interest, dividends, rents, and royalties. Taxable income is gross income minus the deductions allowed corporations, so there is no "adjusted gross income" as is the case with individuals. Note that a company's book income may differ from its tax income. Some book expenses may not be deductible for tax purposes, and certain book income may be exempt from federal taxation. (The corporate tax return has schedules designed to reconcile book income and taxable income.)

Significant differences apply in the tax treatment of capital losses between individuals and corporations. For one thing, corporations are not permitted to claim net capital losses as a deduction against ordinary income; they can be used only to offset capital gains and may be carried back three years and forward five years. On the other hand, corporate taxpayers generally have more recapture of depreciation than individuals, particularly where real estate is involved. In addition, corporations can deduct 80% (100% in the case of affiliated corporations) of dividends received from other domestic corporations. Although the deduction generally is limited to the lesser of 80% of the qualifying dividends or 80% of taxable income, an exception applies where the full deduction yields a net operating loss. (Note: under the Revenue Act of 1987, the 80% dividend-received deduction for corporations is reduced to 70% if the recipient corporation owns less than 20% of the voting power and value of the payer's stock.)

Another deduction available to corporations is for expenditures required to organize the corporation. Under the law, a corporation may elect to amortize organizational expenditures over a period of 60 months or more, if the election is made in a statement attached to the corporate return for its first tax year. (Organizational expenses include fees paid to the state of incorporation, accounting and legal services in organizing the corporation, and expenses incurred at organizational meetings. Nonqualifying expenses such as those associated with selling the stock are ordinarily added to the capital account of the corporation. Expenses incurred only in the first year are covered.

Corporations are permitted to deduct charitable contributions of not more than 10% of its taxable income, computed without regard to the dividends-received deduction or any net-operating-loss or capital-loss carryback. Any contribution in excess of the 10% limitation may be carried forward to the five succeeding tax years. A cash-method corporation may deduct contributions only in the year made, while an accrual-method corporation may elect to deduct contributions authorized by the board but not paid during the tax year if made within $2^{1}/_{2}$ months after the close of the tax year. A deduction will not be allowed if any of the net earnings of the organization that receives the contributions are used for the benefit of any private shareholder or individual.

The tax return must be accompanied by a statement that the resolution authorizing the contribution was adopted by the board during the tax year for which the return is filed. The statement must be signed by the president or other principal officer.

With the foregoing points in mind, one can now understand how corporate income is computed and how net operating losses can result. Generally, such a net operating loss of a corporation may be carried back three years and forward five years to offset taxable income for those years. The corporation can elect to forgo the carryback and to carryforward the loss. This rule is intended to allow companies to average income and losses over a period and to reduce wide disparity in tax treatment from year to year. However, the 1986 Act limits the amount of net operating losses that can be used when there is a change of ownership resulting from purchases of stock, issuance of stock, redemption of stock, etc., of more than 50% of a company's value. The testing period for this purpose is ordinarily three years. In such cases, the net operating losses may not be applied against the taxable income exceeding the value of the company's equity multiplied by the long-term tax-exempt rate for the day of the change of ownership.

This key was intended to highlight some of the changes wrought by the 1986 Act as they affect the choice of entity decision. All in all, the net effect of such changes is to encourage the use of pass-through entities such as partnerships and S corporations. For many businesses, however, the regular C corporation is still attractive.

29

TWO SPECIAL
TAX PROBLEMS

Both the accumulated earnings tax and the personal holding company tax are of keen interest to the closely held
regular C corporation.

The **accumulated earnings tax** basically provides that a
corporation that shields its shareholders from tax liability by
accumulating profits instead of distributing them may be
subject to tax. The tax is imposed where there is an intent to
avoid shareholder income and where the accumulations are
beyond the reasonable needs of the business.

The tax is imposed on accumulated taxable income, which
is taxable income after certain adjustments minus dividends
and the accumulated earnings credit. (For this purpose, the
accumulated earnings credit is the lesser of the reasonable
needs of the business or $250,000 [$150,000 in the case of
personal service corporations].) This tax is in addition to any
other tax due.

A good-faith belief in the need for the accumulation will
generally prevent imposition of the tax. An important issue is
whether the accumulations exceed the reasonable needs of
the business. Generally, the corporation must formulate plans

that are specific, definite, and feasible rather than vague, uncertain, or postponed indefinitely. The plans should be recorded in minute books and reflected in appropriate correspondence. The regulations identify a number of needs that should meet this test such as:

(1) plans to acquire another business
(2) bona fide expansion of the business
(3) replacement of property and equipment
(4) retirement of debt
(5) bona fide business contingencies
(6) redemption of stock
(7) pending litigation
(8) changing business conditions
(9) working capital needs

As regards this last item, the conventional formula for determining whether working capital needs are reasonable is known as the *Bardahl* formula, which permits an accumulation equal to the costs of operating the business for a single operating cycle. (This cycle is often referred to as the amount of time necessary to convert cash into raw materials, raw materials into finished goods, finished goods into sales and receivables, and receivables back into cash.)

Certain corporate actions tend to indicate unreasonable accumulations of earnings. For example, the acquisition of assets unrelated to the corporation's business and the existence of large amounts of cash or other liquid assets would favor imposition of the tax, as would loans to shareholders or to their friends or relatives. Corporations that pay no dividends are suspect.

A tax problem often confused with the accumulated earnings tax is the **personal holding company tax,** which was enacted to discourage incorporated "pocketbooks" from accumulating passive-type income. For example, a personal service corporation might be formed by a talented individual, who would draw a modest salary. The corporation would contract the talent's services out at the going rate so that the difference between the amount received by the corporation and the salary paid could be accumulated in the corporate treasury against a time when earnings would diminish. The personal holding company tax was developed therefore as a penalty tax to discourage such devices, and is currently levied at the rate of 28% of undistributed personal holding company income on top of the regular corporate tax.

For a company to be considered a personal holding company, two tests must be met. First, more than 50% of the fair market value of the outstanding stock must be owned by five or fewer individuals at any time during the last half of the tax year. Thus, many closely held corporations will qualify, especially since very broad constructive ownership rules apply (e.g., stock owned by a corporation, partnership, estate, or trust is considered as owned proportionately by its shareholders, partners, or beneficiaries). Second, under the tainted income test, 60% or more of the adjusted ordinary gross income (exclusive of capital gains) must be derived from personal holding company income. Personal holding company income is basically investment-type income such as rents, royalties, dividends, and annuities as well as income from certain personal service contracts.

If either of these two tests is failed, the tax will not be imposed. One solution might be to disperse stock ownership. Another is to reduce personal holding company income or to increase adjusted ordinary gross income so that the 60% threshold would not be reached.

Another recurring problem relates to corporations in the process of liquidation, at which time their operating income may be substantially reduced. By the time the corporation realizes that it has become what the IRS regards as a personal holding company, it may be impossible to issue a deficiency dividend, which is the basic remedy to avoid imposition of the tax. It should be noted, however, that a corporation may sell its assets and continue as a private investment company for the benefit of the shareholders. To avoid imposition of the tax, such a company would need to pay out its net earnings as a current dividend or, if it is intended that earnings be retained, invest in tax-free bonds.

30

STOCK TRANSFERS

In most publicly held corporations, the transfer of stock from owner to owner is a routine matter. But in closely held corporations there are generally some restrictions on stock transfers, in order to maintain the essential unity and integrity of the enterprise.

Shareholders in a closely held corporation may wish to restrict transfer (i.e., retain the power to choose future associates) for a host of reasons: preventing a competitor from buying shares, avoiding the loss of tax status, providing a market for the shares, or preventing one owner from purchasing a majority of the voting shares outstanding. Such restrictions on transfers make it possible to preserve the partnershiplike status of a close corporation. Hence, the courts will usually enforce restraints that are not unreasonable and that serve a legitimate purpose.

Such restraints are valid and enforceable if the owners' consent to the restriction is found, expressly or impliedly, in the corporation's articles or bylaws, or in an agreement. Further, a transferee of a share of stock is bound by such restrictions if he takes the shares with notice of the restriction.

Under the RMBCA, the articles, the bylaws, or an agreement among shareholders or between the shareholders and the corporation may impose restrictions on the transferability of shares. The restriction will not affect shares issued before the restriction was adopted unless the holders are parties to the restrictive agreement or voted in its favor. Such a restriction is valid and enforceable against all holders if the restriction is noted conspicuously on the stock certificate or is contained in a separate information statement. The RMBCA provides that a restriction on transferability is authorized:

1. To maintain the corporation's status when it is dependent on the number or identity of its shareholders;
2. To preserve exemptions under federal or state securities laws;
3. For any other reasonable purpose.

When reviewing a share-transfer restriction for reasonableness, the courts consider a variety of factors, including the size of the corporation, the degree of restraint, the duration of the restriction, the likelihood of harm to the corporation should the restriction not be upheld, and the efficacy of the restriction in relation to stated corporate purposes.

The RMBCA provides that such a restriction may:

1. obligate the shareholder first to offer the corporation or other persons an opportunity to acquire the restricted shares;
2. obligate the corporation or other persons to acquire the restricted shares;
3. require the corporation, the holders of any class of its shares, or another person to approve the transfer of the restricted shares, if the requirement is not manifestly unreasonable;
4. prohibit the transfer of the restricted shares to designated persons, or classes of persons, if the prohibition is not manifestly unreasonable. As is the case with pre-emptive rights, "shares" includes a security convertible into, or carrying a right to subscribe for or acquire, common stock.

31

STOCK-PURCHASE AGREEMENTS

There are basically two kinds of stock-purchase agreements — stock-redemption agreements and cross-purchase agreements.

Stock Redemption. Under a stock-redemption agreement, any shareholders who desire to transfer their stock must first offer the shares to the corporation. On the death of a shareholder, however, the agreement obligates the corporation to buy, and the estate to sell, the stock. Statutory limitations may apply. First, a corporation's purchase of its own shares may be made only to the extent of unrestricted surplus funds. Second, if the corporation is insolvent, or if the sale would render it insolvent, the corporation may not purchase the shares. (See also Key 33.)

Cross-purchase. In a cross-purchase plan, the corporation itself is not a party to the agreement. If the agreement covers sales within the lifetime of the shareholder, it typically provides that shareholders must first offer their shares to the other shareholders (generally in proportion to each holder's stock ownership). Upon the death of a shareholder, the agreement generally obligates the estate to sell, and the remaining shareholders to purchase, the stock of the deceased shareholder. Again, this would be in proportion to the owners' stockholdings.

Combined agreements. In some cases, a combined agreement may be used. For example, the agreement could provide that a shareholder desiring to transfer shares must first offer the stock to the other shareholders. If they do not purchase the full amount, the shareholder must then offer the remainder to the corporation. The same kind of arrangement may take effect at the death of the shareholder. The agreement could provide that stock not purchased by the remaining shareholders would have to be purchased by the corporation.

Whether the agreement be stock redemption, cross-purchase, or a combination, the agreement must have a bona fide business purpose, and careful consideration should be given to whether the corporation or the remaining shareholders are likely to have sufficient funds to exercise their rights or to perform their obligations. Although a number of options are possible (e.g., creation of a *sinking fund*), life insurance is often used for this purpose. This can prove to be very complex where numerous stockholders are involved, since a policy must be obtained on the life of every shareholder. As an example, if there are ten shareholders and they enter into a cross-purchase agreement, then 90 separate policies would be needed. However, in a stock-redemption agreement, the corporation takes out only one policy on the life of each shareholder.

Regardless of the form of the agreement, if properly drafted, the agreement can freeze the value of the owner's controlling interest for estate and gift taxes and avoid the necessity of a valuation of the owner's interest for such purposes, and ensure the orderly transfer of that interest to whomever the owner desires, without an interruption. Note that the agreement creates a market for the shareholder's interest by protecting the corporation's existence as a going concern, and the remaining shareholders are also spared apprehension over the future.

32

PREEMPTIVE RIGHTS

Preemptive rights protect shareholders from dilution of their interests when the board of directors votes to issue additional stock. These rights entitle all holders to acquire a proportionate share of additional shares of the corporation if such new shares would adversely affect their voting or dividend rights. Thus, if a corporation has 1000 shares authorized, issued, and outstanding, of which 100 shares, or 10%, are owned by Jones, and if the articles are amended to increase the authorized shares to 1500, and all of the 500 additional shares will be issued, if Jones has a preemptive right, he will be eligible to buy 10% of the additional shares (here 50 shares). Of course, Jones must pay whatever price the board in the exercise of its business judgment has established for the shares.

Note that a preemptive right does not force a shareholder to purchase the shares. However, a failure to exercise one's rights within a reasonable amount of time following receipt of notice may constitute a waiver of the right, but only as to the offered shares. Once a shareholder waives a preemptive right, the corporation may generally sell the shares to anyone. Preemptive rights are especially important in closely held corporations, since the majority interest may attempt to "freeze out" the minority interest (see Key 38). In such a freeze-out, the minority shareholders' interests are reduced to relative unimportance against their wishes. Preemptive rights are far from a panacea, however. Thus, minority shareholders can be frozen out if they do not have the money actually to purchase the shares. Further, where a number of shareholders are involved, the effect of preemptive rights on future operations should be considered before including a provision for them in the articles.

Preemptive rights vary according to state law. As these laws now stand, some states favor preemptive rights while others allow them only if there is a specific provision for such rights in the articles of incorporation. The RMBCA provides that the shareholders do not have the right to acquire a corporation's unissued shares except as specified in the articles. The RMBCA makes it clear that a statement in the articles that "the corporation elects to have preemptive rights" (or words to that effect) means that the following principles shall apply except to the extent the articles provide otherwise.

1. The shareholders of the corporation have a preemptive right, granted on uniform terms and conditions prescribed by the board, to acquire proportional amounts of the corporation's unissued shares upon the decision of the board to issue them.

2. Shareholders may waive their preemptive rights and a waiver evidenced by a written statement is irrevocable even if it is not supported by consideration.

3. There is no preemptive right with respect to shares issued as compensation, shares issued to satisfy conversion, option rights created to provide compensation, shares authorized in the articles that are issued within six months from the effective date of incorporation, or shares sold otherwise than for money.

4. Holders of shares of any class without general voting rights but with preferential rights to distributions or assets have no preemptive rights with respect to shares of any class.

5. Holders of shares of any class with general voting rights

but without preferential rights to distributions or assets have no preemptive rights with respect to shares of any class with preferential rights unless the shares with such rights are convertible into, or carry a right to subscribe for or acquire, shares without preferential rights.

6. Shares subject to preemptive rights that are not acquired by shareholders may be issued to any person for a period of a year after being offered to shareholders at a consideration set by the board that is not lower than the consideration set for the exercise of the preemptive rights. An offer at a lower consideration or after the expiration of a year is subject to preemptive rights.

A safer approach is to ensure that all shareholders in the corporation have a veto power over any increases in stock.

A sometimes overlooked point in the area relates to previously authorized but unissued shares that are later offered for sale. Some jurisdictions have held that preemptive rights do not apply to such shares, even though selling such shares means that the minority shareholder's interest will be reduced. However, if the purpose of the sale is to freeze out the minority interest, a court may still declare it to be illegal.

33

REDEMPTION
AND REPURCHASE
OF SHARES

At some point in the life of a corporation it may be desirable for the directors to authorize redemption of some or all of the corporation's issued stock. Since the terminology of *redemption* and *repurchase* is often confused, it is worth clarification here.

Redemption. A corporation may acquire some portion of its outstanding shares by paying a redemption price to the shareholders, who in turn surrender their certificates. Note that redeemed shares can only involve certain classes of stock, generally with the idea of retiring shares with dividend preferences so as to benefit the common shares. If there is only a single class of shares outstanding, it is generally not redeemable, since this would give the directors the ability to eliminate the shareholders to whom they are responsible.

Where a corporation is permitted to redeem less than all of a class of shares outstanding, ordinarily this must be done either proportionately or by lot among all shares subject to redemption. That is, it cannot be done on a discriminatory basis. In any event, once the corporation does give notice that it is calling in a class of shares, the call is irrevocable. Thus, the holders of the called shares become creditors of the corporation, entitled to enforce their claims as creditors. A corporation ordinarily has the power to redeem its shares only when expressly provided in the articles.

The holder of redeemable shares is not a creditor but a shareholder and cannot force the redemption (e.g., if the corporation lacks the necessary funds for the redemption). In any case, the redemption price (i.e., issued price plus a premium) may be fixed in the articles or by the board. Generally, this price must take account of dividends in arrears as well as accrued dividends.

Repurchase. It is not necessary that there be a proviso in the articles giving the corporation the power to repurchase its own shares, since a corporation is generally empowered to acquire, hold and dispose of (but not to vote) its own shares. Although many jurisdictions have limitations that preclude the corporation from using such power unfairly, a corporation is free to repurchase its shares on a nondiscriminatory basis. Repurchased shares that do not have to be canceled (i.e., shares reacquired out of surplus) do remain issued as treasury stock until resold or canceled, with the right to vote, to receive dividends, and so forth, when subsequently sold. This is in contrast to redeemed stock, which is canceled and withdrawn. Note that treasury shares may themselves not be voted or counted for a quorum. Once the corporation decides to purchase its own stock, it must provide notice to the shareholders, asking them to submit tender offers or fixing a price. The shareholders may also be invited to sell just a percentage of their shares.

Under the RMBCA, the concept of treasury stock per se has been eliminated. All shares reacquired by the corporation are treated as authorized but unissued shares. Of course, such shares are not entitled to vote or to receive dividends. If the articles should prohibit the reissuance of reacquired securities, the number of authorized shares is reduced by the number reacquired, effective upon the amendment of the articles. Articles of amendment may be adopted by the board without shareholder approval and are delivered to the secretary of state's office for filing, setting forth the name of the corporation, the reduction in the number of authorized shares, and the total number of authorized shares remaining after reduction of the shares.

As a related matter, a corporation may at any time integrate into a single instrument all of the provisions of its articles and any amendments to the articles that are then in effect. Subject to state law, such restated articles can be adopted by the board without a vote of the shareholders. The restated articles are to be executed, acknowledged, and filed in the same manner as are articles of amendment. After the restated articles are filed, the corporation's previous articles are superseded and the restated articles are the articles from that point onward.

34

STOCK REDEMPTIONS: TAX IMPLICATIONS

If a corporation redeems its stock under specified conditions, the redemption will be treated for tax purposes as a distribution in full or part payment of a shareholder's stock. This kind of stock redemption is defined as an exchange between a corporation and a shareholder of the corporation's stock for property. The shareholder's tax liability on a redemption is the same as if he had sold his shares to a third party.

The primary tax advantage of such redemption treatment is that the shareholder can recover the amount invested in the stock without dividend consequences. Thus, whereas a dividend is taxable as ordinary income to the extent of earnings and profits, exchange treatment means that only the gain is taxed — as a long-term capital gain. As a result of a redemption, the earnings and profits account of the corporation is reduced by an amount not to exceed the taxable share of earnings and profits of the distributing corporation attributable to the stock redeemed. If the corporation distributes appreciated property to the shareholder in the redemption (or, for that matter, as a stock dividend), the corporation is taxed on the distributions. If the corporation realizes a loss by distributing property, this is generally treated as a capital transaction, not subject to loss recognition. Note further that expenses incurred in a redemption are nondeductible capital expenditures. Also nondeductible are such expenses as stock purchase premiums and legal, accounting, transfer, brokerage, and appraisal fees.

Under Section 302 of the tax law, there are four ways to avoid unfavorable dividend treatment for a redemption. First, a redemption will be deemed to be not essentially equivalent to a dividend if it results in a meaningful reduction of the shareholder's proportionate interest in the redeeming corporation. Thus, if all shareholders get essentially the same thing, the redemption will be treated as a dividend.

Second, a "substantially disproportionate distribution will not be treated as a dividend." In such cases, after the distribution, the shareholder must own less than 80% of his total proportionate interest in the business before the redemption. In addition, after the distribution the shareholder must own less than 50% of the total combined voting power of all stock. (Note that the effect of the cut-back requirement cannot be frustrated by a planned series of redemptions.)

Third, if a stockholder terminates his entire interest— voting and nonvoting, preferred and common—through a redemption, the redemption will also qualify for exchange treatment. It is apparent that such a termination would satisfy the substantially disproportionate test mentioned above. In addition, the former shareholder must file an agreement to notify the IRS of any acquisition within a ten-year period and must retain all necessary records relating to the redemption during that period.

Fourth, a redemption in partial liquidation is not a dividend. To qualify, any distributions must be made within the taxable year in which the plan is adopted or within the succeeding year. The basic point of this exception is that shareholders receiving assets in a partial liquidation should receive the same exchange treatment as shareholders in a complete liquidation. If multiple businesses are each operated in distinct corporations, one of the businesses can be liquidated in a nondividend transaction.

Section 303 of the tax law provides that redemptions used to pay death taxes qualify for exchange treatment. Otherwise, such redemptions might qualify as dividends. This rule provides an executor a way to redeem the stock of a closely held business when the stock represents a substantial part of the gross estate of the shareholder-decedent. Thus, the estate can be provided with needed liquidity and be protected from losses in a forced liquidation of property in order to raise needed cash. After a redemption, corporate surplus can be used to pay personal estate costs.

The redemption price is ordinarily the basis of the stock. There are several conditions that have to be met in order to withdraw corporate cash or property to redeem a deceased shareholder's stock in a Section 303 redemption. For this kind of sophisticated estate planning, it is best to consult a qualified adviser.

35

SECTION 1244 STOCK

A related issue to S corporations is the Section 1244 option. As a general rule, any loss sustained on the sale, exchange, or worthlessness of stock is treated as a capital loss deductible only against capital gains and, at the most, $3000 of ordinary income per year. However, under Section 1244, a domestic small-business corporation may issue stock that will qualify as Section 1244 stock so long as certain procedures are satisfied. Owners of such stock are entitled to take an ordinary-income deduction for any loss sustained on its sale, exchange, or worthlessness. The loss deduction limit is currently set at $50,000 in the case of a single taxpayer and $100,000 in the case of married taxpayers filing joint returns. Thus, a taxpayer who acquires Section 1244 stock at a cost of $80,000, then sells the shares later for $5000, has an ordinary loss on a separate return of $50,000 and a capital loss of $25,000. (But note that on a joint return the entire $75,000 loss would be considered ordinary.)

In computing the taxpayer's loss on the sale or exchange of stock, the adjusted basis of the stock is generally compared with the amount realized. Although the yearly limit for loss deduction is as stated above, more than this amount can qualify if the loss is taken over a period of more than a year by spreading out the sales of stock.

In order to qualify as a small-business corporation, a company must have equity capital of not more than $1,000,000. (Fair market value of the corporation's stock is *not* considered.) The stock must be issued for money, for property other than stock, or for securities, and the corporation must be actively engaged in a trade or business. Although both Subchapter S and Section 1244 refer to small business corporations, it should be emphasized that the requirements of each are totally separate and additional to the requirements of the other.

The benefits of Section 1244 are available only to two types of taxpayers: an individual who received the stock in issuance from a small-business corporation and is sustaining the loss, or an individual who is a partner in a partnership that received the stock in issuance from a small-business corporation. Section 1244 is not available to a partner who in turn sells the stock himself. To claim a deduction under Section 1244, the individual or the partnership sustaining the loss must have held the stock continuously from the date of issuance. The benefit of Section 1244 is not available on stock issued to a corporation, trust, or estate.

Section 1244 loss treatment is not available if more than 50% of the corporation's gross receipts during the five tax years before the loss were derived from passive income, such as interest, dividends, rents, annuities, and similar sources. This gross-receipts requirement only applies if the corporation's receipts equal or exceed its deductions other than those for a net operating loss and for dividends received. Further, stock acquired through an investment banking firm or from another person participating in the sale of an issue may qualify for ordinary-loss treatment only if the stock is not first issued to such firm or person. Thus, if the stock is transferred to another, it loses its Section 1244 character, and assuming the holding period is met, it is treated as a short-term capital loss.

Although there is no statutory requirement to this effect, it would appear advisable to have the shares qualifying under Section 1244 be represented by different certificates from those that do not. Interestingly, stock issued on or before July 18, 1984, had to be common stock in order to qualify for Section 1244 treatment, whereas after that date either preferred or common stock can qualify.

Before the 1986 Tax Reform Act, combining Section 1244 with the S election could give a shareholder the best of both worlds. By taking advantage of the S election, shareholders could deduct operating losses currently and offset such losses against income derived from other sources. In addition, Section 1244 gave shareholders maximum tax benefits from losses resulting from the sale or worthlessness of their stock. For tax years beginning after 1986, however, the passive-loss rules require that S-corporation shareholders who do not materially participate in the operation of the business may not deduct losses until they dispose of their stock. Passive shareholders cannot use loss pass-throughs to shelter income from nonpassive sources (be it active income, like salaries, or portfolio income, like dividends). Generally, passive shareholders are only able to offset their losses against income from other passive investments.

Nevertheless, it may still be advisable to qualify stock under Section 1244, so that any loss not recognized currently from corporate operations but instead on a sale or exchange of stock will be allowed as an ordinary-income deduction. Further, Section 1244 qualification offers a backup position for taking an ordinary loss in the event the S election is terminated or deemed ineffective for some reason. In this connection, it is worth emphasizing that nothing is lost by qualifying stock under Section 1244, since it exacts no cost for the benefit given and no penalty for failing to qualify. Gains are still capital gains, as Section 1244 applies only to losses. Further, a Section 1244 loss is regarded as a business loss, hence is deductible from ordinary income. Thus, it is generally a good idea to issue stock on a Section 1244 basis.

36

REORGANIZATIONS

A reorganization is a readjustment of corporate ownership or structure and occurs when a corporation merges, or is bought out, or changes its capital structure, name, form, or place of business. Generally, reorganizations entail exchanges between corporations or between a corporation and its shareholders. From a tax point of view, in most reorganizations, shareholders and other parties to the deal may make exchanges without recognition of gain or loss.

Generally, there are seven types of reorganizations eligible for tax-free treatment:

(1) Type A: statutory merger or consolidation
(2) Type B: acquiring another corporation's stock
(3) Type C: acquiring another corporation's property
(4) Type D: transfer of assets to another corporation
(5) Type E: recapitalizations
(6) Type F: mere changes in identity, form, or place
(7) Type G: insolvency

The Type A reorganization includes both mergers and consolidations. A merger entails the union of two or more corporations in which one of the corporations (the survivor corporation) retains its corporate existence and absorbs another (the transferor corporation). Thus, the transferor is absorbed into the survivor and the transferor's shareholders become shareholders in the survivor. A consolidation is accomplished when a new corporation is formed to take the place of two or more corporations, which then lose their corporate existence by operation of law. In both forms, shareholders and creditors of the disappearing transferor corporations automatically become shareholders and creditors of the transferee corporations.

A merger begins when the board of each corporation adopts an agreement or plan of merger and submits the plan to all shareholders for approval. (Many statutes require approval by two-thirds of the outstanding shares rather than a bare majority.) Note, however, that a merger between a subsidiary and a parent can be accomplished without a shareholder vote where the parent owns a specified percentage of the shares. This is called a *short-form merger* and can be accomplished simply by resolutions adopted by the boards of both corporations. In a short-form merger, the minority shareholders of the subsidiary are entitled to receive the fair value of their shares. Further, some statutes do not require approval by the survivor corporation's shareholders if the stock issued to shareholders of the transferor corporation does not constitute more than a designated percentage of the outstanding shares of the class of stock, and if the merger does not require any change in the survivor's articles of incorporation.

The Type B reorganization entails the acquisition by a corporation of the stock of another corporation *solely* in exchange for its voting stock. Immediately after the acquisition, the acquirer must be in control of the acquired corporation. The control level that must be reached by the acquirer is a minimum of 80% of the total combined voting power of all classes of stock entitled to vote and at least 80% of the total number of shares of all other classes of stock. The Type B reorganization dispenses with the need for shareholder meetings, and dissenters have no right to demand the appraisal value of their shares. State and local merger requirements are inapplicable.

The Type C reorganization involves the acquisition by the

acquirer of substantially all of the assets of the acquired corporation solely in exchange for voting stock (i.e., an exchange of assets for stock). Although there is no precise definition of what constitutes "substantially all," ordinarily assets representing at least 90% of the fair market value of the *net* assets or at least 70% of the fair market value of the *gross* assets held by the acquired corporation must be transferred. Whether a particular percentage meets the requirement depends largely on the nature of the assets retained by the transferring corporation. Thus, if the retained assets consist only of cash or other liquid assets that will be used to discharge liabilities, the percentage of assets can be less than would otherwise be necessary to satisfy the requirements of the law. An exchange will not qualify as a Type C reorganization unless the acquired corporation distributes to its shareholders all the stock, securities, and other properties it receives in the reorganization, in addition to any of its own property that is left. Note that in the Type C reorganization, unlike the Type A, the acquirer assumes only those liabilities it wishes to assume (i.e., it is not liable for unknown or contingent liabilities.) However, where the acquirer assumes a liability of the transferor corporation for the principal purpose of avoiding federal income tax, or if the assumption is not made for valid business purposes, then the total amount of liabilities assumed will be considered money received in the exchange. Further, the assumption of a transferor's liabilities may, in certain cases, so change the character of the transaction that the reorganization will be disqualified.

The Type D reorganization entails the transfer of all or part of the assets of one corporation to another when the transferor, or one or more of its shareholders, is in control of the transferee corporation. Substantially all of the property must be transferred to the second corporation. The Type D reorganization can be either a corporate combination or a corporate division. If it is a corporate combination, control means ownership of at least 50% of the total voting stock or 50% of the total value of all classes of stock. If it is a corporate division, control means ownership of at least 80% of the total voting stock *and* at least 80% of the total number of shares of all other classes of stock. There are a number of reasons why a corporation might effect a corporate division, from antitrust concerns to corporate disputes.

The Type E reorganization or recapitalization entails a change in the amount and character of outstanding capital stock or the paid-in capital of the corporation. In the closely held context, the principal shareholders could recapitalize the company and then give nonvoting common stock to their children (and/or grandchildren) while retaining the voting preferred stock for themselves. This enables the principals to keep both income and voting control while passing on to the family all future appreciation in the value of the business. This estate-freezing technique was substantially eliminated in the 1987 Revenue Act through the enactment of new Section 2036(c). This section provides that if a person has a substantial interest in an enterprise and transfers property having a disproportionately large share of the potential appreciation in this interest while retaining a disproportionately large share of the income of, or rights in, the enterprise, the retention of that interest is equated with a retained life estate. For example, assume Jones recapitalizes a controlled corporation, creating both common and preferred stock and, following the recapitalization, transfers half the common stock to a family member. Since the common stock carries with it a disproportionate share of the appreciation, it will remain in the owner's gross estate for estate tax purposes. (Note: Had Jones transferred half of each class of stock, the transfer would not return to the gross estate because it would have carried with it a proportionate share of the appreciation.)

Some elaboration would be in order. As regards the requirement of holding a substantial interest, this means that at least 10% of the voting power or income earned (or both) in an enterprise must be owned directly or indirectly by the decedent or his family. Although the term "enterprise" is not defined in the law, the committee reports suggest that it includes a business or other property that may produce income or gain; this appears to be broad enough to include real estate.

Turning to the requirement that there must be a transfer of a disproportionately large share of retained earnings, the decedent effectively must have transferred a disproportionately large share of the potential appreciation in the business. The committee reports indicate that this encompasses any share of appreciation in the enterprise greater than the share of appreciation borne by the property retained by the transferor. This entails comparing the ratio of an individual's interest in the potential appreciation to his total interest in the enterprise before the transfer compared to the same ratio recomputed after the transfer.

Finally, the decedent must retain at the time of the transfer an interest in the income or the rights in the enterprise. These rights include "voting rights, conversion rights, liquidation rights, warrants, options, and other rights of value." The income includes any interest on debt, consultant or director fees, and even intrafamily rents or royalties.

Although recapitalization has been largely eliminated as an estate-freezing technique, other devices, such as the personal holding company, still exist.

The Type F reorganization entails a mere change in identity, form, or place of organization, however effected. If a reorganization qualifies as either a Type A, Type C, or Type D reorganization, and simultaneously as a Type F reorganization, Type F treatment will override. Note that such a reorganization is limited to a single operating corporation. Thus, the tax attributes of the predecessor carry over to the successor, and net operating losses can be carried backward or forward.

The Type G reorganization entails a transfer of all or part of the assets of a debtor corporation in bankruptcy, receivership, foreclosure, or similar proceeding, to an acquirer in a transaction where the securities of the acquirer are distributed in a manner that qualifies for tax-free treatment under the law. The debtor corporation's creditors must receive voting stock of the acquirer equal to 80% or more of the total fair market value of the debtor corporation.

In sum, Types A, B, and C are acquisitive transactions. The Type D reorganization may be used to combine two related corporations, to reincorporate, or to effect a corporate division under Section 355. Types E and F reflect changes in the structure of a single corporation. A Type G reorganization is undertaken pursuant to bankruptcy proceedings.

Generally, a reorganization must be pursuant to a plan adopted in advance by the participants and filed with their tax returns. Though a written plan is not expressly required, such a document serves to identify the rights and obligations of all parties and to list the required steps to complete the exchange. There must be a valid business purpose to the reorganization besides the avoidance of taxes, and, with the exception of Type D reorganizations, there must be a continuity of interest on the part of persons who directly or indirectly were the owners before the reorganization. For more details about this complex matter, consult your tax adviser.

37

BALANCING DEBT AND EQUITY

Investors in a new corporation can receive stock, securities, or other property. Subject to state law, corporate organizers have considerable freedom in determining the corporation's capital structure—be it stock alone or some combination of equity and debt. There are advantages and disadvantages to both these forms of financing. With stock, any dividend payments are taxable to the individual but not deductible by the corporation. With debt, the interest payments are taxable to the individual, too, but are generally deductible by the corporation.

This tax preference in favor of thin incorporation—high levels of debt in relation to equity— is reinforced by the fact that it is permissible for a corporation to accumulate earnings to pay off long-term debt, thereby avoiding the accumulated earnings tax dilemma. From the standpoint of many investors debt is generally preferable to equity since, as creditors, they will not be taxed on the withdrawal of their investment when the corporation repays the debt, to the extent that they have a basis in the investment. From a nontax standpoint, there are advantages, too. For example, in any liquidation the owner–

creditor will be able to share in the corporate assets along with outside creditors. If the investment is in stock, however, his interest will be subordinated to that of the creditors.

Among the disadvantages to the heavy use of debt financing is the fact that a corporation may not be able to meet its scheduled interest payments, and thus be placed in default. Further, excessive debt may preclude the corporation from being able to establish lines of credit with other lenders. Note that, from a tax standpoint, if the corporation should fail, losses attributable to the stock may qualify for ordinary loss treatment under Section 1244 (see Key 35). This should be compared to losses on debt, which are treated as a nonbusiness bad debt. Such losses are subject to short-term capital-loss treatment and thus may be offset against ordinary income only to a maximum of $3000 per year. The distinction here is that a nonbusiness bad debt is one unrelated to the taxpayer's trade or business, either when it was created or at the time it became worthless, thus is deductible as a short-term capital loss, whereas a business bad debt is fully deductible as an ordinary loss in the year incurred.

Another problem with thin capitalization is that the IRS may be successful in recharacterizing the so-called debt as equity. In litigation in this area, courts have tended to take an all-or-nothing approach, so gleaning the relevant factors is important. Five criteria are especially relevant:

(1) Whether there is a written, unconditional promise to pay on demand or on a specified date, a certain sum of money in exchange for adequate consideration in money or money's worth, and to pay a fixed rate of interest;

(2) whether the debt is subordinated to or preferred over other corporate debt;

(3) the ratio of debt to equity;

(4) whether the debt is convertible into stock;

(5) the relation between holdings of stock and holdings of debt.

It is important to note than in order for inside debt to be valid, it must be treated as such. Thus, the instrument should bear interest and obligate the corporation to pay both interest and principal on specified dates. There should be a set maturity date, but if the maturity date is too far in the future, the debt may be treated like equity. Payment should not be contingent on earnings. The debt should be properly recorded on the corporate books and reflected as a liability. If the shareholders' debts are subordinated to those of the general creditors, the instrument will look like preferred stock and is likely to be treated as such. Moreover, if a shareholder has personally guaranteed a loan made by an outside creditor so that the lender is looking primarily to the shareholder for repayment, the debt may be reclassified as equity.

38

FREEZEOUT

In the context of closely held corporations, a majority interest may wish to move from controlling shareholder to sole shareholder status and thus seek to freeze out a minority interest by a variety of actions.

In most jurisdictions, a specified percentage of shareholders can dissolve a corporation. Following the dissolution, the former majority interest could form a new corporation to carry on the business. The minority interest may be able to prevent such a dissolution if the majority's objective — ousting the minority — runs contrary to the best interests of the corporation generally. (A suit would be filed by the minority on behalf of the corporation, rather than on behalf of themselves.) This is called a derivative suit and is distinct from a direct action to redress an injury to one's interest as a shareholder.

Any attempt to freeze out a minority shareholder by amending the articles to take away the voting rights of minority interests can also be resisted, since a shareholder's right to vote is considered a right that cannot be changed without consent. (Note: although some changes to the articles are mere formalities, others may substantially impair the rights of shareholders.)

The majority shareholders also cannot deprive those in the minority, without their consent, of contractual dividend rights. However, they may attempt to freeze out the minority simply by passing on the declaration of dividends. Generally, the declaration of a dividend is within the discretion of the board of directors pursuant to the business judgment rule. Withholding payment of dividends for a long period of time can thus be an effective freezeout strategy, since the majority is denied income and the value of the stock may become depressed. The technique will be especially effective where the minority shareholder is in financial straits and is heavily dependent on the dividend income. If the minority shareholders can show that the dividends were withheld solely to freeze them out, a court may compel declaration of a dividend.

If the dividend oppression caused the minority shareholders to sell their interest in the corporation to the majority shareholder below its true value, however, a different remedy is needed; the court may allow the minority holder, like any other defrauded seller, to rescind the sale or to recover from the majority shareholder as damages the difference between the price received and the fair value of the stock.

Thus, there are limits to the board's ability to omit declaration of a dividend, and a court may grant relief if the minority can prove that the directors abused their discretion by acting arbitrarily, fraudulently, or in bad faith. As one court has put it, "the courts will not allow the directors to use their power oppressively by refusing to declare dividends where the net profits and the condition and character of the business clearly warrant it." To determine if the directors have acted properly, the courts examine such factors as the firm's current and future financial needs and whether there are any indications that the majority shareholders have used their influence to harm the minority, or have particular interests (not shared with the minority shareholders) in keeping dividends minimal. Minority shareholders can avoid this problem from the beginning by executing agreements requiring the declaration of dividends under specified circumstances.

39

DISSOLUTION

Dissolution involves gathering together the corporate assets, paying the corporate creditors, and then distributing the remaining corporate assets to the shareholders. Note that if there are corporate assets that remain when the winding-up phase is complete, such assets "escheat" to the state unless the applicable statutes provide otherwise.

There are two principal methods of dissolving a corporation, voluntary and involuntary. In the case of the voluntary dissolution, state statutes generally require a vote of the board of directors recommending a plan of dissolution to the shareholders. The plan must be approved by a majority or a prescribed percentage of the outstanding shares, and there must be a filing of a certificate of dissolution with the office of the secretary of state. Many states require notice to creditors either directly or by publication. Of course, the courts may enjoin a voluntary dissolution if it is found to be unfair or designed to eliminate minority interests.

Involuntary dissolution may be accomplished by action of the state, the directors, or the shareholders. The state may act where there has been an abuse of authority or where a particular requirement, such as the payment of taxes or of the filing of an annual report, has not been met. The shareholders may bring an action only if a specified percentage of the shareholders concur and there are clearly articulated grounds for dissolution, such as abuse of power, abandonment of the business, or misapplication of corporate assets. Thus, a corporation may be involuntarily dissolved when the directors or those in control have acted oppressively, illegally, or fraudulently toward the complaining shareholders.

As another example, "deadlock" can occur when the board consists of an even number of directors who are equally divided and unable to agree on the management of the business. In the context of the closely held corporation, deadlock often arises when the corporate structure allows a faction of shareholders to hold up an action if they disagree with an aspect of corporate policy. The term *dissension* generally refers to disputes among the shareholders so acrimonious that they make corporate relationships difficult and ultimately interfere with the successful management of the business. Note that dissension may or may not lead to deadlock and, ultimately, dissolution.

Notwithstanding its name, the act of dissolution will not ordinarily terminate the corporation. The reason is that it takes time to wind up the affairs of the corporation, to pay the debts, and to distribute the remaining assets. Under the RMBCA, dissolution begins with the filing of a notice of intent to dissolve; the corporation is actually dissolved only after the liquidation process has been completed. During the winding-up phase, the corporation continues to exist and to have the powers and rights of a corporation reasonably incident to liquidation.

There are some alternatives to the dissolution remedy. Under Delaware law, for example, rather than ending the corporation's existence, a court is permitted to appoint a "provisional director" to serve on the board until the court finds that dissension of the board has ended or that the situation seems hopeless. Another option that is more widely used in the closely held context is to use arbitration to resolve disputes. Again, this does not always work, but it has saved many corporations from a premature demise.

State statutes generally provide the extent to which direc-

145

tors and/or shareholders will be liable to creditors upon dissolution of the corporation. Ordinarily, there is no liability if the procedures for dissolution were carried out in strict conformity with the law. Otherwise, directors may be liable to the corporation or to the creditors for distributions to shareholders without making adequate provision for payment to creditors; to the shareholders for any distribution not in accordance with the terms of their shares; or to creditors, who may be able to pursue assets in the possession of shareholders if the distribution prejudiced their rights. Further, there are occasions where payments made to creditors themselves may be reversed if deemed preferential (see also the applicable state fraudulent conveyance statute). At the federal level, preferential payments occur when a corporation satisfies certain debts to the detriment of other creditors. Moreover, under federal tax law, corporate officers, employees, and others responsible for the payment of certain taxes may be personally liable for unpaid taxes following the dissolution of the corporation. Such tax obligations are generally not discharged in bankruptcy.

40

LIQUIDATION

Complete liquidation of a corporation occurs when the shareholders turn in all of their shares and receive in exchange all of the assets of the corporation, following payment of any debts to creditors, including holders of bonds and notes. Under prior law, a corporate distribution of property, whether in a liquidating or in a nonliquidating distribution, produced neither gain nor loss to the corporation. Thus, a single tax resulted — the corporation's owners reported a capital gain equal to the difference between the value of their liquidating distributions and their bases for their stock — and the shareholders took a stepped-up basis for the assets they received. Although the corporation did not recognize gain or loss on the distribution of assets in complete liquidation, it should be noted that there were possible tax consequences — for example, the recapture of depreciation or the investment tax credit could create taxable income.

With the repeal of this so-called *General Utilities* doctrine in the Tax Reform Act of 1986, liquidating corporations now must recognize gain on such sales or distributions. The result is that the liquidation of a C corporation may result in taxation at both the corporate and shareholder levels (the corporation on the difference between the sale proceeds and its bases in the assets, and the shareholder on the distribution of the after-tax proceeds). An exception applies to liquidations of subsidiary corporations.

Thus, the law generally requires a liquidating corporation to recognize gains or losses on distributions of property as if it had sold the property at fair market value and distributed the proceeds. Determining the fair market value of the distributed property is a question of fact. However, if a shareholder assumes a corporate liability or takes property subject to a liability, the fair market value of the property is deemed to be not less than the amount of the liability even if the fair market value is less than the liability.

As an example, if a corporation sells its assets at a gain of $100,000, a 34% corporate tax will be imposed on the gain, leaving the corporation with after-tax proceeds of $66,000. Once the proceeds are distributed to the shareholders, an additional tax in the amount of 28% or $18,480 is imposed, leaving the shareholders with net proceeds of just $47,520. This is an effective rate of 53%, assuming maximum tax brackets. The result would be the same if the assets were distributed by the corporation in liquidation. Note that under the new law, liquidation of an S corporation or partnership still generally results in a single tax. If the corporation in the above example were an S corporation, only one tax would result, and it would be at the shareholder level. Thus, assuming a maximum rate of 28%, the tax would amount to just $28,000, and the after-tax proceeds would be $72,000 as compared to the $47,520 computed above—a difference of $24,480. (However, there is a tax on the disposition of assets within ten years of the selection; this is the tax on built-in gains.)

In sum, under the general rule following tax reform, all gain or loss realized on the complete liquidation of a C corporation must be recognized by both corporation and shareholder. An important exception is made for the liquidation of an 80%-or-more-owned subsidiary. This provision is complex and should be reviewed by competent tax professionals.

QUESTIONS
AND ANSWERS

What are the major forms of business enterprise in the United States?
The sole proprietorship, in which one person owns the business; the partnership, in which there is an association of two or more persons engaged in business as coowners; and the corporation, in which the entity, an artificial "person," is treated as separate for legal and tax purposes from its owners. Corporations range in size from one-person concerns to vast publicly held corporations.

What do the terms "domestic" and "foreign" refer to in the corporate context?
Subject to certain exceptions, a corporation is formed pursuant to state law and is considered to be a domestic corporation in the state that granted its charter and a foreign corporation in any other states in which it does business. The corporation is considered to be a person for purposes of the Due Process and Equal Protection Clauses of the U.S. Constitution but is not so considered for purposes of the Privileges and Immunities Clause.

What are the principal characteristics of the corporate form?
A corporation has an existence separate and distinct from those who own shares in the corporation (shareholders). The

shareholders elect the board of directors, who oversee the management of the business and appoint officers responsible for its day-to-day operation. Some important features of the corporate form are limited liability, centralized management, perpetual existence, and free transferability of interests.

What does limited liability refer to?
In legal terms, the doctrine of limited liability generally shields the corporate shareholders from the debts and obligations of the corporation. Whereas the sole proprietors and partners in a partnership (excepting limited partners in a limited partnership) have all of their nonbusiness and business assets exposed to business debts and obligations, shareholders generally expose only their investment in the corporation to corporate creditors and others seeking recovery from the business. However, the courts may strip away this limited liability ("pierce the corporate veil") where the shareholders have been using the corporation as their "alter ego" or if the corporation was undercapitalized when it incurred the debts.

How is a corporation organized?
Generally, a corporation is formed by the execution and filing with the secretary of state of the articles of incorporation, which are signed by one or more incorporators. After this filing is accepted or approved, the corporation's internal structure must be completed. This is accomplished at an organizational meeting of the incorporators or of the initial board of directors named in the articles. At this meeting, among the business transacted is the adoption of the corporate bylaws, which govern the internal operations of the corporation. Unlike the articles, the bylaws are not made a part of the public record.

What is a corporation by estoppel?
In a corporation by estoppel, certain persons may be estopped (prevented) from challenging the status of the corporation even though neither de jure nor de facto. Thus, one who has dealt with a purported corporation may be estopped from denying the existence of the corporation and those who hold

themselves out as operating in the corporate form are estopped from denying the corporate status.

What is a promoter?

A promoter is a person who, acting alone or in conjunction with one or more persons, directly or indirectly, takes the initiative in founding and organizing the business or enterprise. Generally, the promoter discovers a business or an idea needing to be developed, locates people willing to make the necessary investment, negotiates the contracts necessary for the operation of the enterprise, incorporates the business, and assists management in starting the operation of the business.

What powers are possessed by a corporation?

A corporation has the express power to perform any act authorized by law or its articles of incorporation. Examples of such express powers include the following: the power to sue and be sued; to have a corporate seal; to have perpetual existence; to appoint officers; to acquire, hold, and dispose of real and personal property; and to conduct business within and without the state of incorporation. A corporation also has the implied power to perform all other acts reasonably necessary to accomplish its purposes and not otherwise prohibited by law.

What does "ultra vires" mean?

An ultra vires transaction is one beyond the purposes and powers of the corporation. A transaction within the purposes and powers of the corporation is said to be intra vires.

What is the difference between a debt security and an equity security?

Corporations are empowered to borrow the money necessary for their operations by issuing debt securities. Such securities create a debtor–creditor relationship between the corporation and the security holder and include notes (which have the shortest term), debentures (which are long-term unsecured securities), and bonds (which are long-term secured securities). Equity securities are shares of a corporation's stock, of which there are two principal types — common shares and preferred shares.

What is a share?
A share represents a shareholder's proprietary or ownership interest in the corporation. Ownership of a share signifies the right to receive dividends as declared by the board, the right to receive a portion of the corporate assets on liquidation, and, if voting shares are involved, the right to vote. Ownership of a share does not entitle the holder to an interest in the corporation generally or to any specific asset of the corporation. Title to corporate assets is vested in the corporation and not in the shareholders individually.

What is common stock?
Common shareholders generally possess voting rights and are entitled to dividends as declared by the board of directors and to a proportionate share in the distribution of assets on the corporation's liquidation. Because of these ownership characteristics common stock generally appreciates or depreciates in price according to how profitable a corporation is.

What is preferred stock?
Preferred stock is a class of stock with a preference over other forms of stock, normally as to dividends, but sometimes as to voting or liquidation rights.

What is a stock subscription?
A stock subscription is an agreement by subscribers to purchase stock to be issued by the corporation. Such agreements may be entered into before or after incorporation. If the subscription is accepted by the corporation, the subscriber becomes a shareholder of the corporation. Unless provided otherwise in the agreement, subscriptions are payable in full or in installments at times determined by the board.

What form must the consideration for the shares take?
Subject to state law, there may be restrictions placed on the kinds of consideration for which shares may be issued (e.g., only for money paid, labor done, or property actually

acquired). Shares issued in violation of such requirements are void.

What price applies to such consideration?
It depends on whether the shares are issued on a par or on a no-par basis. With par-value stock, a fixed or stated value is assigned to each share. Such shares must be sold by the corporation at least at par value; shares sold for less are not fully paid and are said to be watered. No-par value stock, which has no fixed value, was developed to eliminate the problem of watered stock and may be sold at whatever price is found in good faith to be reasonable by the board of directors.

What are the rights of shareholders?
Although shareholders generally do not have the right to exercise direct control of the corporation, they may exercise control indirectly through their voting rights (e.g., electing directors, amending the articles and bylaws, and acting on extraordinary or fundamental corporate actions such as mergers and acquisitions). Shareholders also have more limited rights such as to inspect corporate books and records.

What is the difference between straight and cumulative voting?
Generally, in all issues other than the election of the directors, a shareholder is entitled to one vote per share held. Straight voting would thus allow the holders of a simple majority of the shares to elect all of the directors. To protect the minority interest, the shareholders may be permitted to vote cumulatively for directors. Thus, each share is given one vote for each director to be elected, so that minority holders can vote all their shares for one candidate or one set of candidates.

What does voting by proxy refer to?
A proxy is simply a power of attorney given by a shareholder to someone to exercise that shareholder's voting rights. Generally, unless otherwise provided in the proxy, a proxy will not be valid after the expiration of 11 months, and will be revocable unless expressly made irrevocable or coupled with an interest.

What is the difference between a merger and a consolidation?
A merger is a combination of two or more corporations in which one of the constituent corporations remains in being (the surviving corporation) after absorbing the other constituent corporation. A consolidation is a combination of two or more corporations in which the separate existence of the consolidating corporations is absorbed into a new corporation.

What is the difference between a de facto merger and a short-form merger?
A de facto merger contemplates a transaction that is structured other than as a merger but has the same effect as a merger. Such a transaction will be treated as a merger for purposes of affording shareholders a right to an appraisal (i.e., the right to require the corporation to purchase their shares at an objectively determined value). A short-form merger entails a merger of a 90%-owned subsidiary into its parent. Generally, such a merger does not require a shareholder vote. This should be contrasted with mergers generally, which require board approval, shareholder approval, and filing with the secretary of state's office.

How are corporations terminated?
First, the corporation must be dissolved. It may be dissolved voluntarily before or after it commences business or involuntarily by action of a court or administrative action of the secretary of state's office (e.g., for not filing the required annual report or not paying the appropriate tax). Dissolution does not itself terminate the corporation but merely requires the corporation to cease its business, to wind up its affairs, and to liquidate its assets. Termination results when the corporation's assets have been liquidated and the proceeds distributed.

GLOSSARY

Agency   Legal relationship in which one person, the agent, acts in behalf of another person or entity, the principal.

Articles of Incorporation   Document submitted to a state official—usually the secretary of state—describing the purposes of a proposed corporation and listing the names, addresses, and numbers of shares held by each of the incorporators.

Asset   Anything of value that is owned, especially by a business enterprise. Compare with Liability.

Basis   Original cost of an investment, plus any additional capital invested; used in determining capital gains taxes when the investment is sold.

Board of Directors   *See* Directors.

Bond   Corporate security issued in recognition of a debt, obligating the issuer to pay the bondholder a specified amount of interest, usually semiannually, and to repay the loan's principal at the maturity date.

Boot   Payment given in addition, "to boot," in an exchange.

By-laws   Rules for the governance of a corporation or other organization. The by-laws are not a matter of public record and thus affect only members of the corporation.

C Corporation   Regular corporation, as distinguished from an S corporation.

Capital   Money or other economic goods used to promote the production of other goods rather than being consumed.

Capital Gain   Difference between an asset's acquisition price (its basis) and its selling price, if the latter is higher.

Close Corporation   Corporation owned by a single individual or a close-knit group of family or business associates, which is authorized to conduct business without observing many of the corporate formalities, such as holding annual meetings. Regulations vary by state. *See* S Corporation.

Corporation Association of shareholders created under state law and regarded as a legal person authorized to sign contracts and carry on other business within the powers granted in the Articles of Incorporation.

Convertible In referring to a security, one that is exchangeable for a different security, as a bond for common stock, at a set rate.

Debt Obligation of one party to pay or to render some service or good to another party. Corporate debt instruments include bonds and notes. *See* Equity.

Directors Group of people elected by the stockholders of a corporation to have overall direction of the affairs and policies of the enterprise, including the selection and supervision of the top management.

Dividend Distribution of all or, more generally, part of a corporation's earnings to the shareholders, most often of the form of cash or stock, but sometimes in property.

Double Taxation Effect of federal and some state tax laws, which tax the same shareholder income twice, once at the level of corporate earnings, again at personal income, at the level of dividends that are declared.

Equity Ownership in a corporation, as opposed to debt; common stock represents equity.

Estoppel A legal bar that precludes a person from denying that which he has previously affirmed, or vice versa.

ERISA Employee Retirement Income Security Act, a federal law governing most private pension plans.

ESOP Employee Stock Ownership Plan. Benefit that uses stock to provide deferred compensation and ownership participation in a company.

Fiscal Year Any 12-month, 52-week, or 365-day period in the financial operations of a governmental or business entity.

Foreign Corporation In The United States, an out-of-state corporation.

Fringe Benefit   Supplement to an employee's compensation and generally not included in gross taxable income but deductible by the corporation. Includes insurance, pensions, paid vacations, etc.

Liability   The claims of creditors on the assets of a company.

MBCA   Model Business Corporation Act.

Minutes   Official written record of the proceedings of a meeting.

Novation   Agreement to replace one party to a contract with another party; replacement of older debt or obligation with a new debt.

Par Value   Assigned value of a share of stock, often $1.00; this price does not necessarily relate to market value.

Parent Corporation   Corporation that owns more than 50% of the voting stock in another, subsidiary, corporation.

Partnership   Form of business organization in which one or more people pool their resources and share in the profits and losses of the enterprise. General partners, who manage the partnership, have unlimited liability for the debts of the business, but limited partners, who are only investors, are liable only to the extent of their original investment.

RMBCA   Revised Model Business Corporation Act.

S Corporation   Corporate form authorized by Subchapter S of the Internal Revenue Code, in which profits and losses of a corporation are passed through to the shareholders, as in a partnership.

Sole Proprietorship   Unincorporated business owned by one person, who has unlimited liability for the debts of the firm.

Stock   Share of ownership in a corporation, with a claim on the earnings and assets. Common stock is normally voting stock, unlike preferred stock, which has a prior claim on dividends and assets.

Subscriber   One who agrees, usually in writing, to purchase stock in a corporation.

Treasury Stock   Stock issued by a corporation and reacquired by it, but not canceled.

INDEX